World Peace in Three Years or Less . . . or Else!

World Peace in Three Years or Less . . . or Else!

Here's HELP: Happiness, Enough, Love, and Peace

There is a Genie in each of us wanting to be freed to grant our wishes!

Donald Pet, M.D.

iUniverse

WORLD PEACE IN THREE YEARS OR LESS . . . OR ELSE!
HERE'S HELP: HAPPINESS, ENOUGH, LOVE, AND PEACE

iUniverse books may be ordered through booksellers or by contacting:

iUniverse
1663 Liberty Drive
Bloomington, IN 47403
www.iuniverse.com
1-800-Authors (1-800-288-4677)

ISBN: 978-1-5320-1294-5 (sc)
ISBN: 978-1-5320-1295-2 (e)

Library of Congress Control Number: 2016920094

Print information available on the last page.

iUniverse rev. date: 01/09/2017

Endorsements

You have helped me realize it doesn't matter how much money we make if we don't have a world to live in. We are not going to be in a very good state. I teasingly called you the *Al Gore of the peace world*; the uncomfortable truth about the fact that we are at a precipice at our time in history. You've created the Educational Community to address this issue. I love what you are doing. It's really important that we wake up out of our doldrums. We're asleep not just about war, it's about everything. We can wake up to being human. ... I strongly encourage you to go to the Educational Community. You've got the solutions. We are at a critical time in our history, and I think of this man and his work and the community you are developing. We don't have to live in fear; we can live in peace.

—Jack Canfield
most nonfiction books ever sold (five hundred million)
Chicken Soup for the Soul series, *The Success Principles*

For video interviews between Jack Canfield and Donald Pet, go to www.worldpeace. academy.

***

Don Pet is an amazing man who has developed an organization, a newer way of thinking, to help people think better and more constructively about the importance of world peace and what each person, including yourself, can do to bring about a more peaceful and happy world.

—Brian Tracy
world-renowned motivational speaker

***

In 1967 I was in a lot of trouble. I was facing ninety years in prison. I got involved in Dr. Pet's program in Lexington. My life is definitely a lot better. He has helped many people. The last year I worked in the state, I made $78,000. I wouldn't be in this position. I probably wouldn't be alive. I can't believe this happened to me. I became successful through Dr. Pet's program. I highly recommend you read his book. You'll become your own best friend, you'll be less depressed, you'll be healthier, and guess what? You'll live longer. If you read his book, it will be the best money you've ever spent. If you don't like it, I'll give you your money back.

—Peter
a recovered addict

Visit http://www.worldpeace.academy to view the video sources of the above excerpts.

***

On May 11, 2016, I received this e-mail from Carol Austad, a professor at Central Connecticut State University, who for twelve years has taught the largest peace program in the state with Professor David Blitz:

Dear Don,
Here is a comment from one of our students about your lecture:

One person can truly make a difference; all it takes is one ordinary person to start a ripple effect as they touch the people around them. This ripple, as it continues to grow and expand outwards, can reach millions of people. We met several examples of people this semester who, through their work and their practices, are making an active difference. We have seen individual examples from our community at Central Connecticut State University and we have learned of larger organizations working towards a better world. One clear example of a person on a peace building mission is Dr. Donald Pet of The Educational Community.

Dr. Pet presented to our class his Signature Essay in which he outlines "A New Way of Thinking" (ANWOT) that is able to bring about world peace. His essay and discussion targeted the ways in which we are conditioned to think and seven possibilities to reverse negative thoughts and beliefs. Examples of this included: "replacing either/or with both/and, substituting could for should, and 'I allow' for 'they make me'."

Whether we realize it or not, our thoughts have a profound effect on our outlook. If we constantly tell ourselves negative things we begin to believe that the people around us are inherently bad or out to get us. I found Dr. Pet's word replacements especially useful in terms of college students. How often have I said, "I should do this" or "I'm being made to do this?" Too many times to count. A change in attitude can change everything. What Dr. Pet is asking us to do is so simple; it is just replacing a few words in a sentence. But this alone has the potential to shift an entire country's outlook.

The Educational Community essentially offers the world a free guide to peace, "ANWOT is easy to teach and learn by ordinary people, is evergreen, made automatic and effortless in 30 days of practice … is rapidly made viral by the domino effect." As a society we love anything that is free and works fast, and Dr. Pet recognizes that in his Seven Plus Two Formula. The ANWOT website, available to everyone, covers a plethora of peace-building topics right on the first page. The viewer is able to read essays that explain why we have war and what we can do to stop it. Another article is titled: "Why We Do Nothing: Our Imprisoned Passion for World Peace can be Unleashed," while the seven word switches is available right beneath that.

The "plus two" part of Dr. Pet's formula consists of the two secret love-creation skills: "emotional self-endorsement and the reasonable best measure of self-worth." I find the first part of the two plus formula to be especially important. How often do we pause and praise ourselves throughout the day? And, do we not feel guilty in doing so? It can feel "braggy" or awkward to give yourself a pat on the back but that is exactly what Dr. Pet is asking us to do. He states we need to start giving ourselves "pull ups" instead of put downs. It is easier to point out the things we do not like about ourselves or what we would like to change. Yet, that does us no good. Good mental health is necessary to help others. The second part of his plus two formula instructs us to not base our self worth on the outcomes we measure ourselves by. For instance, do not think: "I'm okay if: He/she loves me, I won, or I got an "A." Instead, measure yourself by your "reasonable best" and learn from your mistakes if you do not always reach your "reasonable best." This way we do not feel bad about ourselves if things do not turn out the way we expect, which is quite often in life.

Dr. Pet ends with the simple truth that we are all a work in progress. This is regardless of age, wealth, or success. Simply, there is always room to grow and expand, which is especially true in terms of peace. I enjoyed Dr. Pet's presentation and I find his work to be promising in his pursuit of peace building. What he asks for each of us to do is quite attainable but revolutionary. It is incredible what simple changes in our thought process can do. [student's course evaluation]

Carol Shaw Austad, PhD, Professor
Department of Psychological Science
Co-coordinator of Peace Studies
Central Connecticut State University
Austad@ccsu.edu

July 14, 2016

Don Pet's concept of self-endorsement is an important and essential development for peace studies. His presentation of this and related concepts to an undergraduate class in peace studies was a call to self-reflection, based on the proposition that each individual can do something to affirm themselves and thereby advance the cause of peace. This makes the concept of peace personal and concrete, rather than impersonal and abstract, as has traditionally been maintained, with little or limited impact. As a student who attended one of his lectures wrote [see above]. I can only concur with this evaluation, and hope that more young people can become acquainted with Dr. Pet's work.

David Blitz, PhD
Professor of Philosophy
Co-Coordinator, Peace Studies Program
Central Connecticut State University

Who Is Donald Pet?

Thank you for your interest in what I'm about: HELP (happiness, enough, love, and peace). Most help is self-help with and through other people. We learn from others' stories, who their teachers were and what they have done. Here is an abbreviated version of my story. Like you, I was born an uncut diamond, shaped by billions of years of history and indoctrinated with the animal instincts that were required to survive in a primitive tribal world. Thereupon I was given a name and patriotic, religious, and political symbols that instilled allegiance to the traditions of my tribe(s) and suspicion of those not of my tribe. I learned the importance of power, which is symbolically expressed as money, titles, and material wealth.

Big for my age, I was recruited to play football. This was a very fortunate event because the coach, Otts Helm, also a high school counselor, called me into his office one day and uttered a few words that became a critical turning point in my life. He said I must go to college. This was a surprise to me, as none of my family had finished high school. I received a wonderful liberal education at Johns Hopkins from exceptional teachers who gladly shared their wisdom. By this I mean it liberated me from the instinct and traditions we each acquire through our initial eighteen years. Education in new knowledge, especially in psychology, philosophy, and religion, taught me to think out of the box. I learned about the machinery of the body at the University of Maryland Medical School and the mysteries of the mind while training in psychiatry at Johns Hopkins Hospital. There, I met my most important mentor, Jerome Frank, MD, PhD, who was then the world expert on the psychological causes of war and peace.

In addition to the eclectic training in different treatment modalities, Hopkins was introducing the "therapeutic community," the concept that the entire staff and environment were important in healing, perhaps more so than the primary therapist. From this experience, I became interested in a newer mode of interactive education, which I named the Genie Seminar. I now believe it is the most effective, enjoyable, easiest, and fastest way to teach the skills of living that we require to be successful in any endeavor. The Genie Seminar is described in this book and elsewhere.

My most important education was the privilege to learn from thousands of patients who allowed me to share their struggles to well-being. When I offered my wisdom, they often came up with better ideas and proved what worked and what didn't. I collected their insights, and with the wisdom of other gurus, I have organized them into a curriculum and recommend the newer means to teach it, the Genie Seminar.

I wrote a $5 million, seven-year staffing grant to develop a multimodality treatment program for substance abuse in the greater Hartford, Connecticut area followed by a $1 million grant to create a Connecticut substance abuse training center for persons in this field, including therapists, law enforcement, judges, attorneys, and community leaders. As a consultant to the Special Action Office of the White House on Drug Abuse, I had the opportunity to review grants and evaluate treatment programs in the United States. I learned that the ability of staff to work together was more important than the particular treatment modality.

I see myself as a collector of wisdom more than a creator. Here are basic assumptions that reveal who I am and what I am about (i.e., my mission and purpose).

- Life is a work in progress that began 3.5 billion years ago. The first cell was preprogrammed to increase in complexity and sophistication, to produce energy and redirect the products of its creativity to benefit the greater system(s) of which it becomes a part. Humankind is the growing edge of evolutionary change comprised of fifty trillion cells, interconnected organs, and parts.
- The human brain is capable of creating symbols and imagination and acquiring knowledge and wisdom of our commonly shared reality. We pass our self-awareness forward to increasingly assume control of our own destiny.
- Love is humankind's symbol to describe directing our energy for the benefit of others and/or our self. In the course of evolutionary change, we progress from a simple expression of love to higher levels of expression: self-centered, egotistical, or narcissistic love when the cell divides mitotically to produce its identical self; parental or filial love when the cell is part of a family; tribal love when sovereign clans require competition for scarce survival resources;

erotic love when the bisexual individual evolves into distinct genders and requires fertilization to procreate; and presently, unconditional universal, global, or agape Christian love as our tribes become one interconnected system.

- Someone discovered fire, another individual the wheel, and creativity expands as we pay new knowledge forward. We don't know most of the names of our earliest heroes, but I can highlight some of mine.

1. Darwin and other scientists discovered we could improve the stories our ancestors created to explain who we are and our purpose. The newer, more scientifically verified story tells us we are born as high-level animals, human beings, and are gifted a newer type of brain that can use symbols. Symbols allow us to discover conceptual reality, such as love and hate, philanthropy and greed, and spiritual Truth and myths. We may elevate ourselves above the animals by adding spiritual wisdom to physical solutions. The assumption that a powerful force, God, created all life on the sixth day six thousand years ago, favors certain tribes, occasionally does magical acts, severely punishes those who disobey by sending them eternally to a very bad place, and rewards those who obey with eternal life in the most wonderful heaven we can imagine was the best our ancestors could understand with their limited knowledge. The newer story indicates we are more than high-level animals. We are humane becomings with a mission and the resources to educate ourselves to create the happy, safe, loving home we want and need.

2. Margaret Mead told us we create most of our own problems because of our young language. The patriotic, religious, and political symbols we initially created support the tribal intentions of our animal brain. They limit us to thinking "Survival of the fittest," "My way is the only right way," and "What works for me and my tribe for here and now?" She said we require updated language that relies more on common sense and spiritual values than instinct and tradition. She reminds us that a small number of thoughtful, committed citizens can change the world. "It's the only thing that ever has."

3. Einstein created the $E = mc^2$ formula that revealed the energy of the sun could be the source of a powerful bomb. He didn't want to share it because he realized that the way higher species had been thinking for over a billion years would lead to proliferation of weapons with ultimate destructive power (WUD) and we would use them to end civilization. Only when colleagues

convinced him what would happen if Hitler got there first, he told our president. The Manhattan Project was created and you know the rest. Einstein told us how to prevent the predicted catastrophe: "... a new type of thinking is essential if mankind is to survive and move toward higher levels."[1]

4. Our evolutionary history is like a relay race. Runners carry the baton so far and then pass it forward to the next person who in turn does the same. We don't know the names of our earliest heroes. Some recent names that come to mind include spiritual leaders such as Abraham, Moses, Jesus, Krishna, Buddha, Mohammad, de Chardin, Gandhi, King, and Mother Teresa; and motivational gurus such as Brian Tracy, Marci Shimoff, Barbara Marx Hubbard, Neale Donald Walsch, and Jack Canfield. The names of the thought leaders who contribute to our civilized world are too numerous to list and are ever growing.

5. Epictetus told us, "Only the educated are free." The more I learn, the greater I appreciate that what I think I know is merely my best assumption. The vast wisdom we don't know is far greater than all we collectively know. The challenge is to educate our progeny to create light where there is darkness.

6. My current passion is to pay forward the collective wisdom I have acquired to the many thought leaders who are expanding our collective wisdom. I want my seven grandchildren, great-grandson, additional loved ones, and humanity to enjoy the opportunities I have experienced in my lifetime; surely I am not alone. My hope is that the 7 plus 2 Formula—seven simple word-switches that rapidly create a newer way of thinking and two relatively secret love-creation skills that teach the Golden Rule—will awaken enough world citizens to transform our world into a happy, loving home filled with the blissful peace we want and need.

Our most knowledgeable citizens and futurists tell us there is still time to make the predicted holocaust a nonevent. We must first wake up and then redirect our collective creativity for the benefit of the one world of which we are a part. This book explains how we can become part of the solution instead of remaining the cause of the problem. We have all we need to proceed to succeed. We need only apply our collective will.

---

[1] The New York Times; May 25, 1946.

What Is the Educational Community (EC)?

The EC is a 501(c)(3) nonprofit corporation created March 2008 by its founder and director, Donald Pet, MD. The mission of the EC is to inspire a movement of one million teachers of Einstein's solution to prevent the predicted human catastrophe and create the sustainable happy, loving, abundant, peaceful home we want and need. Each one, reach many teacher (you!) can initiate a domino effect that will circle the world.

The first EC was created at the United States Federal Narcotics Hospital/Prison in Lexington, Kentucky, in 1967. I was given permission to initiate a therapeutic community by overseeing one building that housed thirty inmates. It differed from the standard protocol in that residents were told they were to help one another and there would be regular educational "behavioral studies" meetings. When asked to name the program, one resident suggested "the community." Another said the title should include "education." Thus, the first EC was born. Regular community meetings focused on understanding behavior and mutual problem solving of life's stresses, including those unique to a prison environment.

The second EC was initiated within the Connecticut substance abuse program. The son of a wealthy family died of a heroin overdose. A week later, a friend of the deceased, who was a pallbearer at the funeral, also died of an overdose. With public outcry and the help of the Commissioner of Mental Health, Ernest Shepard, the legislature authorized a special appropriation to develop DARTEC, Drug Addicts Rehabilitated Through the Educational Community. DARTEC was a residential therapeutic community established at Undercliff Psychiatric Hospital in Meriden, CT. The staff consisted of professionals and recovered drug addicts. (We also persuaded the state legislature to create counselor positions as state employees who could be hired on the basis of life experience instead of academic credentials. Some of these counselors were "graduates" of the Lexington EC.)

I developed a third EC in a private-practice setting utilizing the same principles.

While no formal studies were conducted, tangible results speak to the success of these programs. At eighty-plus years, I am passionate to popularize the 7 plus 2 Formula and wake up our world citizens to the imminent danger from WUD and inspire a movement of the one million heroes—each one, reach many—needed to influence our global tribe of seven billion people. Education in essential life skills through Genie Seminars offers the best hope to create Einstein's solution to the greatest puzzle we face:

"Why do we fill our world with fear, hate, scarcity, and war when we want and need HELP (happiness, enough, love, and peace)?"

The EC curriculum and programs are forever *free* on our websites to everyone, everywhere, anytime so no one will be denied the essential skills to make life wonderful.

www.peace.academy
The best starting point with links to other websites

www.worldpeace.academy
Video introduction to ANWOT

www.EinsteinsSolution.org
Love-creation skills

www.7plus2formula.org
Script, audio, and video versions of the 7 plus 2 Formula plus three books.

www.lovingmenow.org
Brad Shepard's recordings and press kit

www.ANWOT.org
Equivalent to a three-credit college course

All EC content is forever *free*. Donations are tax deductible.

World Peace: PO Box 06128
The Educational Community
East Hartford, CT 06128

Foreword

So frequently it is pointed out that the human race has acquired the means of its own destruction that the shocking fact no longer shocks us. Everyone has heard it but no one takes it seriously; statesmen readily acknowledge the ability of the human race to destroy itself and then proceed to act as though it were not a fact at all.
Senator J. William Fulbright[2]

I am passionate that my family and humanity have the opportunities I have experienced in my 80 plus years. Surely, I am not alone. In over 200 random interviews, respondents say they wish or pray for peace. Most acknowledge they do nothing to bring it about, but all say they would take action if they had an idea of what could work. Releasing such pent up energy will be unstoppable. As a realist and optimist, I believe we can solve the biggest puzzle if we merely set our collective minds and energy to the task. This book is a wakeup call to all concerned about the state of our world. We require a movement of one million teachers of Einstein's most important insight: *The unleashed power of the atom has changed everything save our modes of thinking and we thus drift toward unparalleled catastrophe. ... a new type of thinking is essential if mankind is to survive and move toward higher levels.*[3]

Imagine a world based on cooperation above competition, a world where people support and encourage one another instead of tear each other down, and a world where our children can be educated with love, free of fear. And what if the tools for building world peace are the same tools you can use to make your own life a rich, meaningful, and joyous experience? We can have this world if we want it enough. All it takes is, A Newer Way Of Thinking (ANWOT).

---

[2] Preface to *Sanity and Survival*, by Jerome D. Frank (Random House, 1967).
[3] *The New York Times*; May 25, 1946

When you practice the 7 easy mind-freeing, life-changing, world saving word switches that create ANWOT and experience the 2 secret love creation skills that create the Golden Rule, you will want to pay them forward. Each person (you) can start a domino effect that will circle the world. Make your life really significant. Become a world peace entrepreneur.

Wishing you tons of mental wealth

Donald Pet
Donald Pet

Contents

CHAPTER 1

The Biggest Puzzle

Einstein's Most Important Insight: We Require a Newer Way of Thinking (ANWOT)

When Einstein recognized his $E = mc^2$ formula could unleash the power of the sun, he was reluctant to share it. He predicted a new era of *weapons with ultimate destructive power* (WUD). When colleagues pointed out the consequences if Hitler attained these weapons first, Einstein notified President Roosevelt who created the Manhattan Project.[4] We know the rest. Truman's warning to the Japanese prior to the first bomb was ignored. Citizens were doing their daily activities; they saw a flash of light and they were no more. Still no surrender! It required a second bomb.

The thousands of nuclear weapons created, the equivalent in power of seventy thousand Hiroshima-size bombs, include enough in hair-trigger state to wipe out civilization as we know it.[5] They may be unleashed en masse by the press of a button, by one person's bad judgment, or by a mechanical error. They offer no second chance. The next great war will begin and be over in ten minutes. There is no defense, only prevention.

Credible citizens and futurists, the daily news, the series of wars that define our history, and common sense are sounding the alarm that we are about to make ourselves the first species to deliberately create our own extinction. Yet most of the world's citizens remain asleep. This book is a wake-up call! You will learn the cause of war, the cause of peace, and the simple steps to direct our collective energy so

---

4 The massive organization of talent and resources created the first atomic bomb and WUD.
5 Martin Rees, "Grounds for Optimism," *Bulletin of the Atomic Scientists* (January/February 2007): 35.

our loved ones and humanity may continue to survive and thrive. We must solve the *biggest* puzzle:

> *Why do we fill our world with fear, hate, scarcity, and war when we want and need HELP (happiness, enough, love, and peace)?*

Einstein told us what we must do:

> The unleashed power of the atom has changed everything save our modes of thinking, and we thus drift toward unparalleled catastrophe ... a new type of thinking is essential if mankind is to survive and move toward higher levels.[6]

Einstein recognized that WUD had suddenly transformed the normal way we have thought since our creation into a fatal addictive disease. Multiple tribes have embraced the $E = mc^2$ formula to produce WUD, but all have thus far ignored his solution to prevent their use.

The Educational Community (EC) offers the first and sadly the only comprehensive curriculum that explains Einstein's solution: we require *a newer way of thinking* (ANWOT). The 7 plus 2 Formula elevates the capital of our material-physical intentions from the animal portion of our brain to the puzzle-solving, mental-spiritual intentions of our human brain. Seven simple word switches create ANWOT; two powerful yet still secret love-creation skills teach universal unconditional love (i.e., the Golden Rule). The formula exceeds all the criteria needed to proceed to succeed. It is easy to teach and learn by ordinary people, is evergreen, fun, becomes automatic and effortless with thirty days of practice, creates quick and measurable results, can be rapidly made viral by the domino effect, and is available forever *free* to everyone, everywhere, anytime. This book explains the cause of war, the cause of peace, and how to proceed to succeed. We need only to wake up and inspire our collective will to action.

Learning by trial and error is no longer sane when WUD provide no second chance; one mistake can erase humanity. "Insanity is doing the same thing over and over again and expecting different results." We don't like being told that the way we do things has suddenly been made insane by something we didn't do and don't understand. By rejecting the idea that the "normal" way our world citizens

---

[6] *New York Times*, May 25, 1946.

think is suddenly insane, we miss Einstein's critical insight. We can create a newer way of thinking that redirects the energy of fear, hate, scarcity, and war to produce what we want and need: happiness, enough, love, and peace (HELP).

In this book you will learn why imagination is the most important change in our 3.5 billion years of life on earth; the accurate, new Story of Us; the Genie Seminar means of education for solving the *biggest* puzzle; and the most important discovery: addiction to our *either/or* way of thinking prevents us from freeing the wish-granting genie within each of us to fulfill our wants and needs. The EC's interviews with over two hundred individuals reflect the universal wishes and prayers for world peace, identify the helpless/hopeless attitude that explains why most people do nothing to solve the *biggest* puzzle, and enlighten us to the pent-up, unstoppable energy ready to be unleashed to make a better world.[7]

Einstein recognized WUD would suddenly make the way we think a fatal addictive disease and told us we require a newer type of thinking to prevent the predicted apocalypse. He didn't label the normal way we think, and he didn't explain how to educate ourselves in the newer way of thinking. Labeling a disease is the essential first step to study, understand, and prevent its predicted outcome, which is human extinction. The EC names Einstein's disease *either/or* thinking.

The 7 plus 2 Formula creates ANWOT and the skill to effectively practice the Golden Rule in thirty days, more or less. The formula is an easy, practical solution to awaken us to the *biggest* puzzle. You can also learn the additional pieces of the puzzle that, when connected, sustain the happiness, love, and blissful peace we create. These newer discoveries include the Genie Seminar, a more effective means of education; the recent and more accurate Story of Us; the asymptote, the first universal symbol of our updated story; the Supreme Law of Orderliness and Predictability; *strens*, a collection of proven wisdoms that build mental strength; easy word switches that redirect our energy to preferred outcomes; and most importantly, identification of the new fatal disease, *either/or* thinking, that stops us from processing data in the newer *both ... and* thinking that frees the wish-granting genie within each of us.

For several billion years, from the time the first species developed conscious awareness, data has been processed into two categories: us *or* them, my safe tribe *or* their dangerous tribe, right *or* wrong, good *or* bad (*evil*), and so on. Survival required each member of a tribe to be allegiant to his or her extended family, herd,

---

[7] View samples of video interviews at www.anwot.org/why-we-do-nothing.

or flock. The power to compete and win grew by numbers. Individuals could not survive in a savage environment; ostracism was a death sentence. Repetition of *either/or* thinking over time led to habit, habit to tradition, and tradition to a biologic addiction. Either/or addiction to tribal thinking has been normal and adaptive for survival in the savage environment of our ancestors. Competition between tribes for scarce resources leads to war. The stronger tribe and its values dominate. While each tribe is harmed, both usually survive because their weapons cause limited damage.

Interestingly, *either/or* thinking has been the cause of war, and war has been the cause of peace ... until the losing tribe gains enough strength to start the next war. War has also been a driver of evolution: weak or diseased branches are removed, and what remains blossoms with renewed strength ... until now. The E = mc^2 formula introduced WUD; multiple tribes now proliferate them. Some already say it is their moral and religious right to use them. Addiction to *either/or* tribal thinking was adaptive and sane for earlier species (including our human ancestors) for billions of years. This kind of thinking is still considered normal today, but WUD have suddenly transformed normal into insanity and a deadly disease. WUD do not simply prune; they kill the whole bush! The outcome is no longer a temporary win/lose; it is permanent lose/lose. So-called normal thinking has suddenly become a deadly addictive disease that is about to slay us. How about that!

OMG! The way most of our world population thinks has suddenly become insane, and we don't even realize it. The proliferation of WUD has changed our age-old addiction to *either/or* tribal thinking from being adaptive to suddenly being more dangerous than cancer, AIDs, and the Black Plague. There is no defense against WUD. "War and cure" is no longer to be expected with weapons that kill instantly and offer no second chance. Prevention is required if we want our loved ones to survive and thrive.

The 7 plus 2 Formula is the easiest, quickest, and most enjoyable and effective means to solve the *biggest* puzzle by popularizing Einstein's solution to create happiness, love, and sustainable peace. Seven simple word switches rapidly create ANWOT, which inspires acquiring the two powerful yet relatively secret love-creation skills that put into practice the Golden Rule. This 7 plus 2 Formula is rapidly doable and enjoyable. With consistent practice for thirty days, more or less, you can make ANWOT and the Golden Rule automatic and effortless. Substituting *both ... and* thinking for *either/or* thinking promotes cooperation between tribes for shared benefits because it replaces harmful competition that leads to bigotry, prejudice, and destructive confrontation.

Ignoring the *biggest* puzzle is sentencing our children and other loved ones to everything we don't want for them. We can prevent the predictable human catastrophe by educating our global population to collectively apply our new weapons with ultimate constructive power (WUC): common sense (i.e., ANWOT) and unconditional global love (i.e., the Golden Rule). This book explains that the way our animal brain thinks in two either/or categories is the root cause of the puzzle.

You will learn in plain language the specific collective action needed to create Einstein's ANWOT solution to the *either/or* thinking that perceives the world in opposing categories: *What works for me and my family (my tribe) for here and now? My way is the only right way.* The simple solution is by asking a modern version of the Golden Rule to our puzzle-solving brain: *What works for me and you (my tribe and your tribe) for now and the future?* Answer: *reciprocity.* Additional answers include *civilization, harmony,* and *connectedness,* all of which may be summed up in one phrase: *the Golden Rule.*

The EC recommends you immediately learn the 7 plus 2 Formula provided here[8] and on its free websites.[9] These critical ANWOT (seven) and Golden Rule (two) skills will awaken you to the solution of the *biggest* puzzle and inspire you to acquire a deeper understanding of additional puzzle pieces that sustain happiness, love, and peace. First learn the seven mind-freeing, life-changing, world-saving word switches that rapidly create ANWOT. Proceed to the fun practice of the two most powerful yet still secret skills that create unconditional love until you experience their benefits. When you acquire the skill of loving yourself with the abundance that overflows to enrich others, you will become your own best friend and lifelong traveling companion. You will own the most powerful antidepressant, welcome love from others rather than remaining dependent on it, and learn how to bully-proof your kids. Supercharge your progress by sharing and discussing these powerful skills with others.

You will love helping to start the movement of one million love-creation teachers that we estimate are required to sustain blissful peace of mind and world peace. Every "each one, reach many" teacher of the 7 plus 2 Formula (you) can start a domino effect to circle the world. Take three easy steps: (1) learn the Formula, (2)

---

[8] Pages 52–59.

[9] A good starting point is www.peace.academy that has links to additional sites. The website www.7plus2formula.org offers the formula in script, audio, and video forms plus two additional books for the more dedicated student of ANWOT.

pay it forward with a click on the computer, and (3) ask them to do the same when they thank you.

Insight #1—Imagination: The Most Significant Event in Our Evolutionary History

> Imagination is more important than knowledge. For knowledge is limited to all we know and understand while imagination embraces the whole world, stimulating progress, giving birth to evolution.[10]—Einstein

The cerebral cortex is the part of our brain that makes us "human." Imagination is the specialized function of our evolving cerebral cortex that equips us with abstract reasoning, *a* newer way of thinking operating system (ANWOT OS). ANWOT equips us with puzzle-solving sophistication beyond the animal brain's prewired trial-and-error solutions and its reliance on tradition. I refer to the cerebral cortex as our genie organ to stress its wish-granting function instead of its anatomy. Imagination is our genie organ's means to create a new nonphysical, conceptual, second signaling system that can influence the physical signaling system of our animal brain.

Imagination empowers us to discover our personal identity as a *self.*[11] The addition of *self*-consciousness to consciousness distinguishes us from all other life by the degree to which we engage in *self*-programming, *self*-governance, *self*-mastery, intentionality (free will), common sense, and creativity to attain mental freedom from the forces that initially control us: instinct and tradition, nature and our nurturers, and fate and circumstance.

Imagination awakens us to nonphysical *conceptual* reality, which includes the power of unconditional love, forgiveness, kindness, compassion, cooperation for mutual short- and long-term benefits, and all those skills that transform us from human beings (i.e., high-level animals) into *humane becomings.* Conceptual thinking is the means by which we may attain our highest level of moral-spiritual function: the Golden Rule. Imagination adds mental-spiritual power to the animal brain's excellence in managing material-physical power.

Imagination is the specialized ability of our human brain to create mental pictures

---

[10] Wikipedia.

[11] Note: In this book, *self* designates our conceptual self as interpreted by the human portion of our brain. For example, *self-consciousness* includes the assumptions we make about who we are and what we are about more than our anatomical self.

and put them in a sequence, thus creating a motion picture of action over time. The more accurately each "snapshot" reflects the commonly shared reality, the more accurate the motion picture will be. When the motion picture we create can be consistently repeated by everyone, everywhere, every time, it reflects the scientific method, or the Supreme Law of Cause and Effect.

Imagination has enabled us to discover the Supreme Law of Cause and Effect (the Law). This is the one law that has governed the expansion of energy; it is the one law that everything and everyone must obey from the first day.[12] Every effect has a cause, and every cause is the effect of a prior cause until we reach the uncaused First Cause. There are multiple names for the Law, including the Law of Orderliness and Predictability, Truth, the First Cause, and common sense.

Imagination empowers us to "see" deep and wide; near and far; and past, present, and future. Our animal brain's vision is limited to what is superficial, present in time, and local in space. The more accurately our imagination creates the trajectory of our past, the better we can predict our future. Accurate knowledge of our 3.5-billion-year journey empowers us to take action to prevent what will occur if our new genie organ doesn't intervene. Imagination provides the power to redirect the intentions of our animal brain and tradition. Our new power enables us to add higher-level moral-spiritual intentions to the physical signaling system of our animal brain. Imagination makes us the first and only earth creature with sufficient mental power to join the creative forces that determine our destiny, that of our loved ones, and all that is about us. We have been granted the privilege, opportunity, and responsibility to join the earlier programmers who determine who we are and our future ... or its lack, according to the degree we use our new powers constructively or destructively.

Just 150 years ago, Darwin and other scientists applied the scientific method to verify an updated motion picture of our history. The newer Story of Us is that life on earth began 3.5 billion years ago with a single cell. This simple cell went on to create multiple cells, including groups of cells with specialized functions; then develop complex organs and systems of organs; and eventually create individuals made up of fifty trillion cells, who formed families and tribes. Our current challenge is to create a family of interrelated tribes in which each member contributes his or her creativity for the benefit of the whole.

Conceptual reality verified by the scientific method (i.e., universal common

---

[12] We regularly disobey the Ten Commandments, what many hold as God's commands. No one and nothing escapes the Supreme Law that regulates the orderliness in our world.

sense) allows us to accurately anticipate the future and intervene to direct energy to preferred outcomes. We acquire the power of knowledge by applying universal common sense, but it has been managed by tribal leaders' personal assumptions, which are often supported only by leaps of faith in authority. Imagination empowers us to update our history (i.e., multiple "his" stories by tribal leaders) to a more accurate universal "our" story. The scientific method empowers us to discover our identity and our purpose. The gift of our emerging human brain inspires us to learn we are humane becomings on a mission to elevate ourselves to higher levels of moral-spiritual sophistication.

The animal portion of our brain functions like a mechanical thermostat—mindless and automatic—to effortlessly maintain the status quo. Its sense organs input data from the external world we all share, but they only detect superficial characteristics in present time and local place, and they focus on differences that separate us from them and pit tribe against tribe. Our human brain applies imagination to know our past and empowers us to influence our future. It creates motion pictures to perceive our connectedness and similarities.

This insight explains why we must quickly assume the responsibility to elevate the capital of our intentions from our animal brain to our newly emerging, puzzle-solving human brain; from domination through material-physical might to cooperation for mutual gain, applying mental-spiritual might; from conditional tribal love to unconditional global love; and from "He who has the gold rules!" to the Golden Rule. ANWOT is our means to transform us from high-level animals (i.e., human beings) into humane becomings.

> We can't solve problems by using the same kind of thinking we used when we created them.[13]—Einstein

Insight #2—The Story of Us: "His" Story ➔ "Our" New Story

Our survival urgently requires that we update our multiple "his" stories (history), which separate us, to a more accurate universal "our" story that awakens us to our connectedness. The actions we take are influenced by how we understand ourselves in relation to the world. The slow, hardly perceptible increase in the accuracy of knowledge explains the persistence of multiple "his" stories. Our history reflects the

---

[13] *New York Times*, May 25, 1946.

limited perspective of our animal brain. Lacking the use of symbols to engage in conceptual puzzle solving, the prehuman brain emphasized physical might to attain its intentions. The recent discovery and spread of the scientific method has created an explosion in the speed and accuracy of new knowledge. Knowledge is the source of power that we direct to nuclear, biological, and chemical WUD. We are waking up to how we can make knowledge our source for "weapons" with ultimate constructive power (WUC). WUC include common sense (ANWOT) and unconditional love (the Golden Rule). Common sense is not common, and we preach unconditional love but have yet to effectively teach it.

"His" stories originate and are supported by instinct, tradition, and the authority of male leaders. According to a popular current version of our history, a powerful masculine force known as "God" magically created everything six thousand years ago. Humankind and other creatures were created on the sixth day. He favors males above females and periodically selects a specific male to make known his commands and enforce them. God declares that obedience to his rules will be rewarded with eternal bliss and disobedience will incur eternal damnation. He periodically intervenes to perform magical acts when his favored tribe is in need. Individuals and tribes may receive favors by taking actions that include prayer, sacrifice, rituals, bargaining, and attacking individuals and tribes that do not follow his rules. Among the many names for the primal force throughout history are Yahweh, Jesus, Allah, and Krishna. Men selected to receive God's intention include Abraham, Moses, Mohammad, and the pope. Some leaders, such as Mao, Stalin, and Hitler, claim their source of absolute knowledge is personal intuition. A critical assumption in "his" story is that the world is sharply divided into good and evil. Good must dominate evil through material-physical, win/lose confrontation.

The new Story of Us, the updating of "his" story to "our" story, is based on the recent spread of the scientific method. The exponential growth of science allows us to see deep and wide; near and far; and past, present and future. The updated story reveals that our universe was created fourteen billion years ago. Data collected everywhere, anytime and every time by anyone verifies that life began 3.5 billion years ago with a single cell energized for two innate intentions: (1) to be creative through reproduction and diversification and (2) to direct the products of its energy to sustain the life cycle of each more complex system of which it becomes a part through the process of evolution.

As organisms increased in complexity, they divided into two genders, each having specialized functions focused on perpetuating the species. Male energy was given the special task of survival by using physical power to dominate in competition for scarce resources. Female energy was assigned the special task of birthing and nurturing progeny to reproductive age. Males have traditionally used their physical muscle power to usurp an unequal balance between the sexes. Thus, our history is "his" story.

Circa two million years ago, our brain began a 350 percent growth process, primarily in the cerebral cortex, while other organs remained relatively unchanged in size and function. The human brain is a mere infant compared to the trial-and-error action pathways programmed into the animal brain. The recent increase in intelligence, *self*-consciousness, and conceptual thinking has empowered our species to evolve to higher levels of function.

The introduction of symbols fifty thousand years ago gave us imagination and a personal "*self*" identify. Imagination has immense significance as it empowers the human mind with the ability to create and to add the conceptual powers of *conditional tribal love and hate* to the animal brain's reliance on physical power. There was a considerable gap until *unconditional universal love* was introduced twenty-five hundred years ago.

The creative impulse has gradually evolved to produce complex, multicelled individuals clustered into tribes. The next level of sophistication requires connecting the sovereign tribes into a harmonious global system. Tribal love linked to *either/or* thinking has brought us this far, but the proliferation of WUD to tribes who believe it is their moral and religious right to use them "has changed everything except our way of thinking" (Einstein). Survival through material-physical might was necessary in the savage world of our ancestors to compete for scarce resources. Trial-and-error learning supports dominance through survival of the fittest. Either/or win/lose confrontation applying physical power will prevail until we recognize that conceptual power leading to both ... and win/win cooperation is superior to physical might to solve problems.

Our animal brain is the product of billions of years of trial-and-error programming by a creative force we call fate and circumstance, nature and nurture, instinct and tradition, God, the primal creative force, or some combination. Whichever label(s) we prefer, we are referring to the same creative impulse that sustains our evolution. The prime function of the animal brain is to sustain the body and the life cycle. Like a thermostat, it works automatically to maintain the normal state. The animal brain's way of thinking, or *operating system*, will remain a servant to its first programmer(s) until we educate our emerging *genie organ* in the humane ANWOT skills that free us to become our own person.

Our story continues with the spread of the scientific method three hundred years ago. This enabled the human mind to begin an acceleration of its speed to reach its present explosive rate of expanding knowledge. There are more scientists alive today than in all of history. It took another 150 years before Darwin and other scientists collected the knowledge that made it possible to discover our origins and update the motion picture of our history.

Creativity that challenges established assumptions is frequently ignored or rejected, and the thinker is often punished. Teilhard de Chardin, a Jesuit priest who added a spiritual interpretation to Darwin's scientific explanation of our emergence, was put under house arrest and forbidden to publish his ideas during his lifetime. Now his views are heralded. Even as scientific verification became widespread, the modification of "his" story to the more accurate "our" story was fiercely rejected. Superstitious beliefs, such as witches exist, the world is flat, and Earth is the center of the universe, did not yield instantly. Our story still meets resistance and is unknown to much of the world's population. Tribal love supported by the animal brain's *either/ or* way of thinking is still our dominant way of directing energy.

While our animal brain is highly functional at birth, the human mind requires about two decades to reach physical and emotional maturity. In addition, we require education in *self*-programming and wisdom to partner with the early creative force(s) that determine our destiny, the future of our loved ones, and all that is about us.

The animal brain is duty bound to consistently direct our newer brain's power of knowledge to create more deadly weapons. It processes new data by trial-and-error learning, and has neither the capability to see far ahead nor the patience to apply the conceptual wisdom required for prevention. It will continue to try to solve the *biggest* puzzle with muscle might. Einstein's solution, educating our puzzle-solving *genie organ* in a newer way of thinking, frees our genie from domination by our animal brain. It is our best hope to prevent *self*-inflicted Armageddon. Plotting the critical dates of our evolution on a chart creates an *asymptote*. Linked to meaning the asymptote is an ideal universal symbol of our connectedness. It reflects an accurate motion picture of our new story with equal or greater emotional power than our tribal symbols.[14]

---

[14] See appendix B for our first symbol to accurately call forth "our story."

Insight #3—Education: The ANWOT Skills to Proceed to Succeed

We now have the imagination, wisdom, and technology to rapidly teach ANWOT and the Golden Rule. The EC is the first and, we sadly believe, the only comprehensive curriculum that offers Einstein's solution free to anyone, anytime, and everywhere through its websites and books.

The commonsense curriculum identifies the skills to prevent human catastrophe and create sustainable blissful peace. The Internet provides the means to rapidly educate our world population at little or no cost. The 7 plus 2 Formula skills are made automatic and effortless with thirty days of regular practice, and they can be passed forward with a click on the computer to inspire others. Additional skills, or strens, are required to strengthen and sustain ANWOT and the Golden Rule. They are available at www.peace.academy where you will also find *The 7plus2 Formula* and *The Stren Book*.

Make your life even more wonderful. The Genie Seminar is a newer means of lifelong education in the skills (strens) that make us mental-spiritual millionaires. The updated Story of Us explains in greater detail who we are and our mission as humane becomings. The asymptote is the first universal symbol to accurately tell our story with the emotional power to overcome the patriotic, religious, and political symbols that set tribes against one another. The Supreme Law of Cause and Effect (also known as the Law of Orderliness and Predictability, or the Law) identifies the one commandment that all life and inanimate things must obey, and gives us the ability to forecast the future. The one hundred-plus strens are a collection of wisdoms proven by others to strengthen our thinking, and a glossary provides new terms and word switches that activate the moral-spiritual intentions of our human brain above the material-physical needs of our animal brain.

Education in the scientifically verified Story of Us explains we are born high-level animals, i.e., human beings. We are required to transform ourselves into dynamic humane becomings or become extinct. Evolution is the creative process of growth to higher levels of sophistication. This requires that each unit within the system works for the benefit of the total system. Though the units comprising a system may be very different, as are our organs, each unit must contribute its specialized skills for the greater whole to survive and thrive. The failure of one part, one organ, or one tribe may lead to the death of the whole. Each emergence of greater complexity brings with it the intention to cooperate for mutual benefit. We call this "civilization."[15] When we ask such questions as "Why are we here?" and "What is our purpose?" a reasonable answer is that we have an innate creative impulse to elevate ourselves to higher and higher levels of civilization. Each cell, organ, individual, family, and tribe is part of a larger creative process moving to higher levels of civilization. The driving force for survival is reciprocity, which we express as the Golden Rule. Our updated history reveals that failure to establish reciprocity results in extinction of the species! As today's different tribes become increasingly interrelated, surviving and thriving require newer skills to cooperate above harmful competition to dominate. ANWOT and the Golden Rule add unconditional global love to conditional tribal love.

The new universal Story of Us inspires us to create symbols that update the traditional *either/or* thinking of our animal brain to the more accurate *both ... and* way of thinking of our emerging *genie organ*, which recognizes our connectedness over our differences. A movement of one million "each one, reach many" love-creation teachers is estimated to be sufficient to influence our seven billion earth citizens to direct their energy to create happiness, love, and blissful peace. If one song by a rock star can attract millions to the Internet, we can certainly inspire the necessary teachers of ANWOT and the Golden Rule. The creative power of imagination and new opportunities for mass education has empowered a small group of committed thought leaders to start a movement that will rapidly spread ANWOT and the Golden Rule via the domino effect. Unleashing the pent-up love energy within our global population to collectively solve the *biggest* puzzle will be unstoppable.

Insight #4—The "Normal" Addiction That Is About to Slay Us

Addiction to *either/or* thinking has suddenly become fatal, and we don't know it! Survival requires that we awaken to the new disease that is about to slay us. The proliferation of WUD to tribes who believe it is their moral and religious right to use them "has changed everything save our modes of thinking and we thus drift toward unparalleled catastrophe" (Einstein).[16] Humankind's addiction to our current way of thinking has been normal, sane, and adaptive since the emergence of conscious

---

[15] *American Heritage Dictionary* defines *civilize* as "to bring out of a primitive or savage state; educate or enlighten; refine."

[16] *New York Times*, May 25, 1946

awareness ... until now! WUD have transformed the normal way data has been processed for billions of years to suddenly be insane and maladaptive. WUD are more deadly than cancer, AIDs, and the Black Plague; they are about to make us the first species to deliberately create its own extinction. We now know how to prevent the human catastrophe predicted by our most knowledgeable citizens, and we are very close to doing so. However, our unrecognized addiction to the normal way we think will continue to cause us to act as though this new fatal disease doesn't exist.

The animal portion of our brain functions as a mechanical sorting machine. It separates preferred "somethings" (for example, apples) from less desirable ones. When our human brain remains subservient to our animal brain, it automatically divides our world into "my good tribe" and the "other bad tribe." Like every addiction, until the sufferer is convinced that his or her behavior is a harmful disease, the addictive behavior is protected and the Good Samaritan is rejected as an intruder. And even after that, *self*-control of any addiction usually requires the support of concerned others.

Addiction to *either/or* thinking is the reason we are born with the intention to express tribal love. All complex life forms are instinctively allegiant to their kind and lack respect for anyone or anything not of their tribe. Tribal love is the reason our history is defined by its series of wars. Since the emergence of the cerebral cortex over a billion years ago, species with conscious awareness, such as the dinosaur, have been preprogrammed to instinctively think in two opposing categories. Likewise, with the emergence of the human-type brain over the last two to four million years, the genetically prewired animal portion of the human species' brain continues to think of "me, my family, and my tribe" as separate from "not my kind."

When our 150,000-years-young species, *Homo sapiens sapiens* (literally the human who knows it knows), first created symbols fifty thousand years ago, we began the tradition of using patriotic, religious, and political symbols that intensify tribal love. Personal and tribal assumptions, supported primarily by huge leaps of faith in authority and physical might, are likely to distort who we are and our purpose. The behaviors that follow are likely to be flawed and even harmful. The updated, more accurate Story of Us was discovered and verified by the scientific method and universal common sense just 150 years ago. However, we have yet to create a single symbol that accurately tells our story with sufficient emotion to overcome our multiple patriotic, religious, and political tribal stories.

There are multiple reasons why addiction to the *either/or* way of thinking, which leads to tribal love and war between tribes, has been sane and adaptive ... until now.

Conditional tribal love has been ...

a. **necessary for survival**. An individual could not survive in the savage world of our ancestors. Strength in numbers provides protection and the ability to subdue other species for food that would otherwise not be possible.

b. **an important driver of evolution**. In the absence of common sense, *either/or* thinking requires physical might to compete for scarce resources and settle differences of values. The strongest tribe prevails to assume dominance and pass on its genetics, traditions, and values.

c. **the main cause of peace**. War has traditionally been the cause of peace. Calm is sustained until the weaker group or a different tribe builds strength to wage the next war.

d. **nature's way of pruning what no longer works**. When the dead branches of a bush are removed, the remaining branches bloom with greater vigor. Wars waged with weapons having limited destructive power thin out the ranks of each tribe, but both survive and usually "bloom" stronger.

e. **the highest expression of reciprocity for the animal brain's level of evolution** ... until the emergence of our genie organ. Tribal love is a necessary step to the next sophisticated level of love: unconditional universal love.

WUD have suddenly transformed *either/or* thinking from a normal adaptive addiction into a disease fatal to humankind. We can make the threat of WUD the driver of change, from dependency thinking to the freedom to become our own person by assuming responsibility for our well-being. Effective education that redirects tribal conditional love to universal unconditional universal love (the Golden Rule) can prevent the predicted tragedy. The Golden Rule is readily achieved by popularizing our genie organ's newer *both* ... *and* symbols that process data emphasizing similarities rather than differences.

The next war fought with WUD will likely have the outcome most people resist even imagining: *self*-extinction! "All is fair in love and war." Every available weapon has been used in times of war. Current events, common sense, opinions of our most knowledgeable citizens, and the fact that scholars describe our history by its succession of wars allow us to predict with a high degree of certainty that there will always be another war ... unless we change the way we think.

Survival of humankind requires that we elevate the capital of our intentions from our material-physical animal brain to the puzzle-solving intentions of our mental-spiritual human brain. Addiction to the traditional way we think blocks us from initiating the simple actions that will prevent human catastrophe and create sustainable peace. People are unaware of the urgency to create ANWOT and to teach rather than merely preach the Golden Rule. Of those who are aware, most refuse to do anything about it, just like any other addict. Thus far, war has always been followed by cure. But a cure no longer works with weapons so instantly deadly that they provide no second chance. Citizens in Hiroshima and Nagasaki were going about their customary routine when there was a sudden flash of light and they were no more. Truman's warnings were ignored until after the second bomb was dropped on Nagasaki. Today's equivalents in power of seventy thousand Hiroshima-size bombs are on ready-release status, waiting to be launched by the push of a button or a mechanical error.[17] We will continue on a rapid course to self-destruct until we expose this new, unrecognized deadly disease.

An addiction is the compulsive pursuit of a behavior. Most addictions are necessary to support our well-being, commonly to attain pleasure and/or avoid pain. Complex species are born addicted to instinctive behaviors proven adaptive to survival, for example, breathing, taking in nutrition, crying for help, and learning by mimicking others. Procreation, nurturing progeny, and fight-or-flight behaviors are added as we attain maturity. Healthy addictions ensure the mindless, automatic, and effortless performance of behaviors required to sustain the life cycle until our genie organ acquires the intelligence, imagination, and wisdom to assume personal responsibility for our destiny.

Addictions can be dangerous because they are hardwired and inflexible. When addictive behavior becomes maladaptive, commonly from an unfamiliar challenge like WUD, it can lead to extinction of the host unless a more effective behavior replaces it. The new Story of Us enlightens us that our emerging genie organ provides the willpower to assume the responsibility and opportunity to manage our life's experience. Will we evolve by choice or by chance? Skills that are easy to teach and learn can redirect the addictions prescribed by instinct and tradition to a newer way of thinking that frees us to become our own master. Substituting *both* ... *and* for *either/or* thinking focuses on our connectedness and need to cooperate for mutual gain above competing in win/lose competition.

The wonderful news is that the gift of self-management through the intelligence, imagination, and creativity of our human brain empowers us to prevent the predicted

---

[17] Bruce G. Blair, "Primed and Ready," *Bulletin of the Atomic Scientists* (January/February 2007): 35.

fatal outcome of doing nothing. All life differs from inanimate objects by the ability to create energy that leads to behavior. Humankind is distinguished from other life by the degree to which our human mind applies our gifts to partner with the force(s) that created us. Our specialized genie organ, the cerebral cortex part of our brain—with maturity and appropriate education—assumes responsibility for our life's experience. As we grow the power of knowledge and the power of wisdom through the scientific method, we increasingly free our will to redirect the addictive behaviors that no longer work to better solutions that lead to preferred outcomes.

Thus far in our evolution, humankind has applied tribal symbols to attain the power of constructive and destructive knowledge, which has made our species king of the beasts and ruler on earth. With the emergence of conscious awareness, our young genie organ was fully subservient to the material-physical, "might is right" tribal intentions of the animal portion of our brain. This explains why our first symbols have been and remain primarily patriotic, religious, and political—icons that express tribal love and support win/lose confrontation to establish dominance. We are just beginning to add our genie organ's power of wisdom to direct our new knowledge to unconditional global love.

Our genie organ creates symbols. Symbols (i.e., words and icons) allow us to take "snapshot" pictures, store them, and arrange them in sequence to create motion pictures. A motion picture adds the ability to see past, present, and future; near and far; and deep and wide. When we create an accurate motion picture of our past, we can use that trajectory to imagine the future. This enables us to initiate action that redirects the path of the trajectory to a new outcome we create, instead of the outcome dictated by prior events. We can readily understand this if we picture a train-track engineer redirecting the path of a train to a destination of his choice by changing a single switch. Changing a symbol is often sufficient to change our interpretation of data and switch the direction of energy to a newer outcome. For example, substituting "I can" for "I can't" or "I could" for "I should" or "I allow" for "They make me" can change the way we think, feel, and act. Symbols are our genie organ's source of conceptual mental-spiritual power, as well as our means to free our *self* from addiction to the instincts and traditions hardwired in our animal brain.

Symbols are our source of free will to assume responsibility for our life's experience. They are the means we use to enhance imagination. Imagination creates conceptual thinking. Conceptual thinking is the source of the scientific method. The scientific method is our gateway to universal common sense, Truth, and verifying the importance of moral-spiritual power (the Golden Rule).

17

The secret of elevating the material-physical intentions of our animal brain to the higher mental-spiritual level of our genie organ is the creation of newer symbols that serve the *both ... and* intentions of the Golden Rule: unconditional love, forgiveness, kindness, compassion, cooperation for mutual benefit, and the additional qualities that transform us from high-level animals (human beings) into humane becomings.

The solution to the *biggest* puzzle is very simple: seven easy-to-learn word switches to create ANWOT and two powerful mental skills are sufficient to teach the Golden Rule. But no matter how simple the solution and how close we are to success, the 7 plus 2 Formula will be of no avail if our addiction to *either/or* thinking makes us shun the solution.

The human mind is programmed by forces that have their way with us before our genie organ develops the power of knowledge to resist control by instinct and tradition, and the strength of wisdom to create more adaptive behaviors. Our human brain is an infant compared to the billions of years of trial-and-error learning by instinct and tradition. Sophisticated use of symbols is a mere fifty thousand years old, and the widespread use of the printed word is measured in centuries. Our animal brain is ready to function at birth while our human brain is not physically mature until late in our second decade.

Dictators are rarely willing to relinquish their power. Instinct and tradition, like human dictators, resist attempts to diminish their control. Success in freeing our self to become our own person requires that we must deal with a formidable obstacle. The animal brain and the traditions that have been prescribed and inscribed to survive for billions of years can be expected to resist any attempt to modify what has stood the test of time. Like a thermostat, our animal brain has been programmed with successful adaptations through trial and error to recognize that new claims rarely improve what is tried and true; they more commonly cause problems.

This is why Moses, Jesus, Gandhi, Martin Luther King, the suffragettes, Galileo, Copernicus, Lincoln, Teilhard de Chardin, Freud, Darwin, and most creators of new ways suffer for their originality. Until we recognize the ubiquitous prevalence of addiction to *either/or* thinking, we will not only resist Einstein's newer way of thinking and the skills that teach the Golden Rule, but our establishment also will continue to punish those who dare to challenge tradition.

Our educational, economic, political, and religious establishments are the outcome of addiction to *either/or* thinking, which leads to tribal love and causes us to focus on our differences and support harmful win/lose competition to establish dominance. We cannot expect to elevate tribal love to global love until we recognize and deal with our addiction to *either/or* thinking. The wonderful news is that we now have the knowledge and the means to proceed to succeed. We have been gifted a specialized genie organ capable of freeing us from addiction and creating the practical means to educate the world's citizens in simple skills that elevate our intentions from our animal brain to our puzzle-solving, genie-like human brain. Accurate symbols that awaken us to this deadly, addictive either/or disease offer our best hope to inspire the rally we require to proceed to succeed.

CHAPTER 2

Creating World Peace

Prepare yourself for a startling revelation: we, through our traditional education, are the root cause of the *biggest* puzzle. All of humankind follow some combination of patriotic, religious, and political tribal symbols that divide the world into *our* tribe *or their* tribe. We "educate" our citizens to express allegiance to "our side" and to fear what is "not our side." Our young, emerging human brain is in the *crawling* stage of transitioning the "might makes right" intentions from our animal brain to the reciprocal, moral-spiritual intentions attainable from our newer brain. We are just starting to create the symbols that elevate us from higher-level animals to humane becomings.

Comparing our prehuman animal brain to our newer, emerging human brain reveals the source of the problem and the commonsense actions needed to create a happy solution. The way we think explains why our history is defined by its series of wars, and what we must do to survive and thrive. Commonsense explanations reveal commonsense solutions. The highest intention of the animal brain is attained through material-physical might, while the highest intention of the human brain is attained through mental-spiritual might. The cause of the *biggest* puzzle is revealed when we understand how the animal brain processes data. The animal brain's operating system explains why our history is "his" story. Our newer genie organ's way of processing information discovers knowledge to update our history from "his story" to "our story."

Note: Impatient readers may prefer to skip beyond the explanation of how ANWOT works straight to the curriculum (page 32). Just as driving an automobile doesn't require us to understand the machinery that serves us, learning and practicing the

ANWOT skills will create the desired benefits even if we don't understand how. More dedicated readers will want the greater satisfaction of a deeper understanding of the distinction between our animal brain and our emerging genie organ. This knowledge reveals the creative process of elevating ourselves from high-level animals (i.e., human beings) to humane becomings.

Getting to Know the Animal Brain

The prehuman animal brain is a mass of interconnected cells with specialized functions. Anatomists identify multiple brain centers: the medulla, pons, pituitary, pineal body, cerebellum, and thalamus. Other classifications are made as scientists gain more understanding of the interrelated functions of the billions of cells and trillions of connections that we refer to as the animal brain.

The animal brain has long been the most sophisticated machine we know. We take pride in our ingenuity when viewing a fine Swiss watch or a space rocket, but we are humbled by the intricacy of the brain. It prewires itself in nine months to manage fifty trillion cells and automatically coordinates the specialized functions of multiple organs. At puberty, it can trigger the creation of additional brains by inspiring a few minutes of pleasurable sexual intercourse. Our animal brain is the accumulation of 3.5 billion years of trial-and-error learning that complexified from a single cell into a labyrinth of nerves and electrical and chemical physical mediators. Our prehuman animal brain was the latest and most complex organ to evolve until the emergence of our puzzle-solving genie organ.

The animal brain has been prewired through trial-and-error adaptation to maintain the body in a constant state. Malfunction of any unit may sabotage its mission and lead to extinction. Behaviors that lead to survival are repeated, become habit, and then passed forward to later generations to become tradition. The sense organs that provide information to the brain focus on differences, dividing data into two categories: safe or dangerous, good or bad (evil), us or them (our tribe or not our tribe), and so forth. Either/or processing of data into "the right (good) way" or "the wrong (bad, evil) way" leads to prejudice, bigotry, intolerance, harmful confrontation, and war. Our "his" story is defined by its series of win/ lose confrontations. In time, losers commonly recover and get a second chance. However, the introduction of WUD, which offer no second chance, usher us into a new era where lose/lose confrontation will make us history instead of continuing to make history.

The highest intention of our animal brain is to sustain its self, family, and tribe. Sustaining the life cycle emphasizes procreation through sexual intercourse and protection of progeny to reproductive maturity. Strength grows with numbers, thus the need for tribal affiliation. The animal brain is innately programmed to form tribes. This is also why the language of our animal brain is dominated by tribal symbols. An individual or isolated family could not survive in a savage world. Exclusion from the tribe is a commonly practiced form of severe punishment that once meant certain death. The behavioral pattern to herd or flock with one's kind and mindlessly submit to the authority of instinct, tradition, or a human dictator is prominent within many species. A small dog can control a herd of sheep by a bark or a nip at the leg. Human tribes are similarly preprogrammed to obey the authority of instinct, tradition, and human dictators. The symbols that dominate our language divide us into teams according to a flag, religion, and politics that we are assigned through our formative years. Identifying with a team enables us to combine our collective physical might and more successfully compete for resources. For example, a skillful group can kill a whale to feed itself for a long time. An individual would have difficulty subduing a large or dangerous animal.

The personal truth of the tribal leader becomes the tribal truth, which becomes the tribal law supported by the authority of physical might. King Henry the Eighth changed the national religion of England to "legally" divorce one wife and behead two others. Hitler indoctrinated a country to believe there was one superior race. American soldiers massacred native Indians even after signing treaties with them. Mao and Stalin purged millions of dissenters. ISIS justifies the beheading of individuals who dare to think other than "the one right way." Every tribe creates tribal symbols that support the tribal intentions of the animal brain, usually without regard for others. Common sense and unconditional global love, our newest weapons of ultimate constructive power (WUC), are unknown to the animal brain, limited in our human ancestors, and are just now becoming the focus of greater attention. We are discovering and verifying the essential conceptual skills that transform us from sophisticated animals into civilized humane becomings. The task of our current and future generations is to effectively awaken our population to conceptual mental-spiritual truth, the Golden Rule.

The animal brain's sensory-motor operating system (OS) consists of multiple sense organs[18] that excel in receiving and sorting physical data into separate categories by detecting differences between physical characteristics. However, the animal brain is poorly equipped to address nonmaterial concepts, such as universal unconditional love, forgiveness, justice, and reciprocity. The animal brain's sense organs are attuned to material-physical differences; mental-spiritual similarities are beyond their range. Our animal brains' highest intentions are consciously expressed by patriotic, religious, and political symbols that convey tribal values. Energy directed to benefit "our side" is often at the expense of non–tribe members. Prejudice (prejudgment), bigotry, and intolerance are the inevitable manifestations of either/or processing of data.

The Animal Brain's Education

Animal brain education begins soon after conception. It consists of behaviors programmed through nerves and chemicals acquired by trial and error over billions of years. By birth, the animal brain is already "educated" (indoctrinated) with the prescribed behaviors proven to work in the uncivilized environment of our ancestors. Intentions are wired by some combination of genes, instinct, emotion, and tradition. They are active at birth and meet limited resistance from our immature and uneducated human brain.

The indoctrination that begins prior to birth is intensified through our formative years. Our genie organ is gifted with extraordinary skill in rote learning from birth through puberty. It is a *tabula rasa* ("unwritten on tablet") ready to be inscribed easily into the beliefs and assumptions of our nurturers. This is why children learn languages so easily. Tradition explains why tribal allegiance resists yielding to common sense. Learning is dictated by specialized prescriptive symbols that serve as triggers to initiate a predetermined action, for example, "should," "must," "have to," and "ought." A combination of patriotic, religious, and political tribal symbols sorts data into two categories—our way or their way. Blind allegiance is encouraged.

> Patriotism is, fundamentally, a conviction that a particular country is the best in the world because you were born into it.—George Bernard Shaw

---

[18] The best-known sense organs are the ears, eyes, tongue, nose, and skin, corresponding to hearing, sight, taste, smell, and touch.

Non–tribe members are commonly dehumanized, especially during war. The dominant process of education leads to the assumption, "My way is the only right way." The teacher provides the "correct" information, and the student learns to repeat it on demand. Original thought that contradicts authority is disregarded and often punished. The prewired and hardwired intentions prominent in our animal brain will continue to pursue win/lose confrontation to assert dominance, even though this way of thinking has been made obsolete by the discovery and proliferation of WUD. The animal brain's process of either/or education is most prominent in countries led by a male dictator, where knowledge and mental freedom are limited to the laws established by the leader's authority, irrespective of common sense.

With the introduction of imagination to consciousness, the animal brain became aware of conceptual symbolic reality. The concept of "infinity" leads to greed. Enough is no longer enough. Newly sought imperatives include excessive pursuit of money, fame, titles, "toys" that impress, and eternal life. Masculine energy is directed to dominance, winning, and becoming the master. Feminine energy esteems physical attractiveness and nurturing, especially children. Conditional love, kindness, empathy, and the higher-level humane skills are directed to self, family, and tribe because the animal brain is limited to *either/or* thinking. Unconditional global love must wait for self-consciousness and education to mature in a newer way of thinking that elevates the capital of our intentions from our animal brain to our emerging cerebral cortical brain. Lacking education in ANWOT, we understand that survival is a contest of "either my way or the wrong way." The tribe's way is the only acceptable alternative. "His" story is set in stone until a new tribal leader decides to revise the tribe's history to suit his personal truths and biases. Previous idols and idolized leaders are commonly erased by new tribe leaders. Creative perspectives that contradict tradition and the tribal leader, even if verified by common sense, are ignored or punished.

Once programmed, the animal brain remains loyal to its early programmer(s). The features of animal-brain education include sexual reproduction; protection of progeny; maintenance of the body's physiology and resistance to change; triumph of good over evil *(either/or processing of data)*; tribal loyalty (the herd instinct); obedience to the authority of instinct, tradition, and human dictators above common sense; *self*-aggrandizement; ascribing magical power to a leader; and short-term gain at the cost of long-term pain. Originality is squashed in the dogmatic process of authoritarian education.

However, rote learning is a necessary prerequisite to the mental freedom we need to become our own person. Teaching the three Rs—reading, writing, arithmetic—and common safety precautions, such as "Don't go in the street," are examples where prescriptive education equips us with the basic skills necessary to later add *both ... and* thinking to *either/or* thinking. Rote learning is an appropriate, effective process to instill universal knowledge that has already been verified by the scientific method (i.e., common sense).

Knowledge provides the building blocks for the creative process. Creativity is built on knowledge. However, dogmatic education set by the personal preferences of a tribal leader obstructs the creative process by substituting prejudice and bigotry for knowledge. Educational content, including physical, conceptual, and spiritual values, needs to be subject to evaluation, interpretation, and verification by common sense. Personal conceptual values are less likely to be universally verified this way.

Getting to Know the Human Brain: Our *Self*, Our Genie Organ

The cerebral cortex is the most recent part of our brain to evolve. *Cortex* means "outer covering." Its emergence two million years ago makes it an infant compared to the 3.5 billion years of trial-and-error action pathways programmed into the animal brain. This newer portion of our brain gives us a personal identity with many new features: *self*-programming, *self*-mastery, *self*-governance, *self*-intention, imagination, thought control, mental freedom from instinct and tradition, and the creativity to apply these special qualities to transform us from human beings into humane becomings.

For these reasons, I refer to the cerebral cortex as our genie organ. The transformation of our species from high-level animals (i.e., human beings) into humane becomings began about fifty thousand years ago with the introduction of symbols to enhance language, and the greater use of imagination. These new skills added *self*-consciousness to conscious awareness. Imagination is the tool of our emerging genie organ that empowers us to discover, share, record, grow, pass forward, and apply the power of knowledge to become creators of nonphysical conceptual reality. Imagination adds moral-spiritual might to the animal brain's reliance on material-physical might. The emergence of *self*-consciousness makes us the only species equipped with sufficient commonsense knowledge of conceptual reality to actively determine who we are and what we will become.

Intelligence, imagination, intentionality (free will), and conceptual thinking are our special tools for modifying existing programs and introducing original ones. Our genie organ creates symbols to enhance our imagination, which awaken us to commonsense conceptual reality. Imagination equips us for mental puzzle solving, including prevention. It empowers us to become increasingly creative and destructive. It creates snapshots and puts them in sequence to create a mental motion picture trajectory reaching from our past to the present. This allows us to intentionally overrule prior programmers to influence who we are and change our future. We may cause a predictable but undesirable event to become a nonevent, what we call "prevention." We are no longer bound to follow the script of our past programmers. Our conceptual *self* increases our share of influence in the partnership with nature and nurture in proportion to the speed we acquire and popularize accurate knowledge of cause and effect (i.e., the scientific method).

Our emerging genie organ represents the latest degree of programming sophistication. ANWOT updates our animal brain's "his" story to a more accurate "our" story. The human mind is at the growing edge of the evolutionary process. As we expand the power of knowledge, we increasingly assume the responsibility and the opportunity to create our future and that of our loved ones ... or its lack. Imagination plus the power of knowledge positions us to modify the animal brain's prewired intentions. Unlike other life that is bound to follow the script of instinct and tradition, our human mind is equipped to become partners with fate and circumstance in determining our destiny.

Don't forget this essential understanding: *Self*-consciousness, with its puzzle-solving, wish-granting ability, joins consciousness as a slave to the intentions of the animal brain until the unfolding of two events: (1) our genie organ attains a high degree of physical maturity, and (2) it receives education in specific ANWOT mental skills.

The future of civilization depends on educating our genie organ in ANWOT to add commonsense wisdom to instinct and tradition. Until we free the puzzle-solving genie residing within our human brain from domination by our animal brain, it will continue to serve the highest intentions of instinct and tradition. We will continue to function as high-level animals until we popularize education in the ANWOT skills that transfer the capital of our intentions from our animal brain to our puzzle-solving human brain.

Our Genie organ's Sensory-Motor "Magical" Operating System (OS)

Our genie organ manages data very differently from the animal brain. Imagination, the genie-like "magical" power of the human brain, converts physical signals into concepts, initiates new combinations, and then chooses one to transform back into a commonly shared reality. When a person shows us an empty hat, says "Abracadabra," and pulls out a rabbit, we call him or her a magician. When the trick is revealed, the entertainer is called an illusionist. Our genie organ routinely transforms physical reality into a nonphysical concept and then reverses the process to "pull out" an original physical or conceptual product. Scientists have yet to understand the magic of this creative transformation.

Our genie organ creates concepts and plays with alternative actions, mentally rehearses them, and then applies abstract logic before choosing which idea to willfully convert into physical action. Imagination is our genie organ's magic wand to grant us both material-physical and conceptual wishes. Examples of material-physical products include automobiles, computers, art, music ... and bombs. Examples of mental-spiritual (nonphysical) products include love and hate, freedom and slavery, philanthropy and greed, and purity and contamination. Unconditional universal love is a newer concept that elevates conditional tribal love to a higher level of evolution. Transforming ourselves into humane becomings includes education in unconditional universal love, forgiveness, kindness, justice, compassion, cooperation for mutual gain, and all those conceptual qualities embraced by the Golden Rule.

Our genie organ creates symbols and energizes them with meaning that introduces a newer nonphysical, *conceptual* second signaling system capable of influencing the *physical* primary signaling system of our animal brain. The power of meaning becomes a trigger that can activate the final pathway to action. The sensory system of our genie organ consists of specialized cells that receive raw data and link it to a symbol, such as a word or icon. Earlier programmers, such as instinct and nurturers, assign either/or symbols that emphasize differences. Our genie organ is capable of adding *both ... and* symbols that emphasize conceptual reality and similarities. Imagination is the transformative component in this new conceptual sensory-motor OS. Simply calling forth the designated symbol can activate the primary physical OS of our animal brain.

With maturity and education, our *self*-programming genie organ becomes a cocreator with other programmers, for example instinct and tradition, which have had their way through our years of immaturity when we were powerless to resist.

Self-consciousness and *self*-programming add new features to consciousness. Imagination, abstract reasoning, common sense, and wisdom are capable of recognizing and applying the power of mental-spiritual reality to *self*-mastery. Earlier programmers and human dictators will continue to determine who we are and what we become unless they are challenged by the mental-spiritual power of ANWOT.

The ANWOT OS excels in the use of imagination to see deep and wide, past and future, and local and distant. These new features awaken us to the benefit of cooperation for mutual gain, instead of competition to assert dominance. The power of *conditional tribal* love that mobilizes destructive energy to dominate other tribes yields to the power of *unconditional universal* love to bring about cooperation and reciprocity. ANWOT is our means to progress from savagery to civilization. Our new story perceives the world as an emerging "us *and* them" continuum instead of the dualistic "us *or* them" world of the animal brain. Focus is directed to similarities over differences.

The high-level function of our genie organ connects individual parts to reciprocate for the mutual benefit of the total system, thus puzzle solving. Challenges are addressed as puzzles to be solved by group intelligence instead of domination by win/lose confrontation. The generic puzzle-solving question of our genie organ is "What will make things better for me and you (my tribe and your tribe) for now and the future?" This newer version of the Golden Rule overrules the animal brain's inflexible problem-causing sentence that leads to win/lose confrontation: "What will make things better for me and my tribe for here and now?" and "My way is the only right way!"

Two New Symbols: Trigger Words and Word Switches

The ANWOT OS that is needed to solve the *biggest* puzzle is elusive because our young language lacks symbols suited to move the intentions of our animal brain to the highest intentions of our genie organ. We have created many symbols (words, icons, flags) that express the win/lose, survival-of-the-fittest tribal intentions of our animal brain, but we have yet to popularize a single symbol that conveys our need for unconditional universal love. Symbols are designed to remain loyal to their programmer(s). New symbols energized with meaning and emotional energy are required for ANWOT to overcome the prevailing animal-brain way of thinking.[19] Trigger words and word switches are two such symbols.

A *trigger word* is a symbol or combination of words that turn on the prewired intentions of our animal brain. A *word switch* is a symbol that has the power to redirect the energy of a trigger word to turn on the higher-level intention(s) of our genie organ. Word switches are our tools to create ANWOT.

Our genie organ introduces a second signaling system by creating word switches to mentally "switch on" our primary physical signaling system. Trigger words serve the intentions of our animal brain; word switches serve our puzzle-solving genie organ. Just as our organs have specialized functions, our animal brain and genie organ each create specialized symbols to serve themselves. Our first language, "baby-talk," is made up of the symbols that serve the authority of our animal brain. The slow process of the individual and collective maturing of our genie organ progressively awakens us to ANWOT and its many benefits.

Consider these examples of the use of word switches:

1. Replacing "either/or" with "both ... and." This is a critical substitution because it focuses on our commonalities above our differences.
2. Consistently substituting the puzzle-solving question "What will make things better for me and you (my tribe and your tribe) for now and the future?" directs action to cooperation instead of confrontation when using the problem-causing sentence, "What works for me and my tribe here and now? My way is the only right way."
3. Substituting the descriptive word "could" for the prescriptive word "should" replaces the command for a predetermined action and invites our genie organ to create better alternative solutions supported by common sense.
4. Substituting "I allow" for "He (she, they, it) makes me ..." redirects energy from the animal brain's blaming response to assume personal responsibility.

Just as changing a single train-track switch can reroute the direction and destination of the entire train, a symbol—a single word switch—empowers our human mind to modify thinking, feelings, and action. Word switches are our means to alter the course of fate and circumstance. By doing this, we not only create the outcome we prefer but we also prevent the predetermined path and destination

---

[19] The Educational Community introduces a new universal symbol. See appendix B.

that leads to what we don't want. Word switches lead to a creative, puzzle-solving, newer way of thinking supported by common sense. They redirect the prewired traditional solutions that worked in the past but may have become maladaptive when facing new challenges.

By awakening to the universal law of cause and effect (i.e., the Supreme Law of Orderliness and Predictability), anyone can become a mental-spiritual millionaire. Mental-spiritual millionaires, unlike many material-physical millionaires, consistently make a wonderful life—even when the world is unfair—and they love giving away their wealth to others. Word switches and strens,[20] such as those provided on the Educational Community's free websites, are required to elevate our thinking. As few as one hundred word switches are enough to sustain the upgrade to ANWOT, to free our wish-filling genie from domination by our animal brain, and to shift the capital of our intentions to our puzzle-solving genie organ.[21]

The recent upgrading of "his" story to "our" story based on the scientific method reveals that the mission of our intelligent genie organ is to prepare humanity to reach its highest level of function by teaching the skills of self-governance and civilization that benefit all world citizens. This supersedes the animal brain's primary intention, which is to preserve life for "us": one's self, family, and tribe.[22] Civilization is best achieved by educating ourselves in ANWOT and the Golden Rule skills that elevate us to humane becomings (content) and popularizing Genie Seminars to unite our creative energy to do good (process).

The Genie organ's Process of Education

Liberal education frees the intelligent, commonsense, puzzle-solving genie organ from its initial slavery to our animal brain. Dogmatic animal-brain education is most pronounced in fundamentalist tribes, and least pronounced in highly civilized tribes where mental freedom and creativity in the arts and sciences is encouraged. Historically, animals and people who were indoctrinated early in life remain limited

---

[20] *Stren* is another new vocabulary word switch that indicates any wisdom, insight, concept, or experience that strengthens ANWOT.

[21] The essays "Anwot Concepts" and "Glossary of Terms" (www.anwot.org) offer one hundred word switches and new meanings to upgrade our present thinking to ANWOT.

[22] The emergence of self, family, and tribe is reflected in the emergence of newer expressions of love, progressing from narcissistic → filial → tribal → erotic love. The next level of sophistication in love expression will be unconditional global love—if we succeed in popularizing ANWOT.

in knowledge and wisdom and passively submit to the instinct and traditions of our early programmers. Mentally freeing our genie to become our own person is among the highest priorities of our genie organ. Once freed from instinct, tradition, and human dictators, the genie will grant wishes guided by universal common sense rather than tribal law. The moral-spiritual intentions of our genie organ, supported by universal consensus, will be assigned a higher priority than the tribal intentions of the animal brain, which are supported by local and usually masculine authority.

While our animal brain favors didactic education, our genie organ wants us to create better solutions. The status quo is open to examination, and innovation is welcomed. This newer form of education relies on universal, collective common sense above obedience to a designated tribal authority whose law is absolute. ANWOT encourages the joy of puzzle solving. Self-governance through personal and shared creativity replaces the dependency we all experience during our formative years. The teacher shares information to explore its meaning and create new practical puzzle-solving alternatives. The curriculum includes knowledge verified by the scientific method (i.e., content) that can be repeated by anyone, anywhere, anytime through common sense, and explores issues by seeking everyone's perspectives (process).

Essential Takeaways of the Updated "Our" Story

Our newer story requires volumes when properly told. The essential knowledge awakens us from the stupor of our prehuman brain to the wisdom of our puzzle-solving genie organ. We all start life with a relatively similar preprogrammed animal brain adapted to survive in a savage environment. Then we are taught how to think, feel, and act from human instructors and circumstance. Our early education may include the ANWOT skills to become our own person, punishment to thwart any attempt to free our self from earlier masters, or anything in between, depending on our nurturers. Unlike other life forms, our human mind offers us a puzzle-solving, genie organ that is capable of education in *self*-programming.

CHAPTER 3

Solving the Biggest Puzzle: ANWOT Education and the Genie Seminar

The commonsense explanation for the cause of the *biggest* puzzle reveals its commonsense solution: education in the essential newer way of thinking (ANWOT) and love-creation (the Golden Rule) skills offered within the Genie Seminar.

The Genie Seminar is a tool for continuous, lifelong education. It is an interactive method to teach and learn the strens (skills, success principles) we require to survive and thrive. Through social intercourse, the Genie Seminar promotes cooperative approaches to answering the questions of what people want and need: happiness, unconditional love, abundance, and peace. In each seminar, small doses of the ANWOT skills are presented via some combination of script, audio, video, or short live presentations. Each meeting will address one or more of the critical basic strens required to establish the newer way of thinking. Once the essential ANWOT curriculum is covered, members are encouraged to introduce their own original strens, those proven by others to be effective, or to repeat core-curriculum strens. A group facilitator is prepared through simple pointers to lead participants in a productive discussion on the practical application of the topic. Members may volunteer to facilitate the seminar.

The seminar is conducted in the fashion of a *self*-help group, Alcoholics Anonymous being an excellent model. The essential difference is that these meetings begin with one of the mental-strength-building concepts (strens) that serve as the topic for discussion. (Lay volunteers may lead Genie Seminars at negligible cost.) They are suited for multiple venues: schools (educational), churches (religious), businesses, prisons, libraries, and homes. They can be especially effective when used in primary schools to promote ANWOT skills and social competence, prevent bullying, and detect tendencies of "shooters"[23] so early preventive intervention can be arranged.

The Genie Seminars offer important secondary benefits as well as ANWOT education. They provide an exciting method of learning. Members bond, provide mutual emotional support in the course of sharing, and develop trust, friendship, and companionship in a safe setting that ensures the longevity of the group. Since most individuals only begin to develop *self*-programming in their late twenties, the seminar is a wonderful opportunity for ongoing, lifelong education.

Education in ANWOT is necessary to free our genie and become our own person. It transfers the capital of our intentions from our animal brain to our newer human brain. Imagination is the magic wand that empowers our genie organ. It is the tool that helps us come to a conclusion that can be attained and repeated by anyone and everyone, anywhere and everywhere, anytime and every time. Connecting knowledge like the pieces of a jigsaw puzzle creates a mental motion picture that accurately lets us see who we are and what we may make of ourselves. As we update "his" story to "our" story, we discover our interconnectedness to a common source and to one another. The new story reveals a path from an either/or, us or them world of conflict to a *both ... and* world where *them* disappears, leaving only *us* to share the joyous, loving, abundant, peaceful home we can cocreate. Most of our world population continues in the *either/or* way of thinking that WUDs have suddenly transformed into a silent, fatal disease about to slay humanity. The survival of humankind requires those of us who attain a higher level of thinking to provide ANWOT education to our less fortunate brothers and sisters.

On the highest level, the intentions of our animal brain and our emerging genie organ are the same: surviving and sustaining the life cycle. However, the human brain adds collective, commonsense puzzle solving to attain win/win reciprocity to the animal brain's highest intentions, which emphasize physical win/lose confrontation. ANWOT education elevates mental-spiritual might above material-physical might, female status to the equivalent of male status, unconditional universal love above conditional tribal love, cooperation for mutual gain above win/lose confrontation for shared pain, and wise creeds and good deeds above greed and speed. ANWOT balances female nurturing might with male physical might as our puzzle-solving

---

23 There is a growing incidence of mass shootings such as Sandy Hook, Connecticut where a student killed 26 people including 20 primary school children.

genie organ awakens us to the wisdom of our higher-level intentions—as expressed in various iterations of the Golden Rule.

We continue to submit to the authority and traditions of our animal brain and neglect the problem-solving, commonsense wisdom calling out from our genie organ. We are sentencing our children and other loved ones to everything we don't want for them unless we awaken from our stupor. Their fate is our cause. Will you become part of the solution and not remain part of the problem?

Teach Happiness, Love, and Peace: Ten Puzzle Pieces

Make your life *really* significant. Newly discovered insights, when joined together, strengthen Einstein's solution for us to have what we want and need: HELP ➜ happiness, enough, love, and peace. This is explained in the EC's gift to you in our forever *free* websites and books.

1. **The essential action**: The 7 plus 2 Formula is the most effective, enjoyable, easiest, and quickest way to wake up our global population. It combines ANWOT and the Golden Rule in a practical format.

   a) Seven simple mind-freeing, life-changing, world-saving word switches are sufficient to popularize Einstein's solution to the *biggest* puzzle: "We shall require a newer way of thinking (ANWOT)." They elevate the capital of our intentions from our material-physical animal brain to our moral-spiritual human brain. These mere seven word substitutions are essential to prevent the predicted human catastrophe and create permanent peace.

   b) The two most powerful yet still secret love-creation skills—*emotional self-endorsement* and *the reasonable best measure of self-worth*—effectively teach instead of merely preach the Golden Rule, which is our highest moral-spiritual standard to guide our thinking, feelings, and actions. Modern versions include "What will work for my tribe and your tribe for now and the future?" and "Love myself with the abundance that overflows to enrich the world."

   Inspiring a movement of one million teachers of the 7 plus 2 Formula offers our best hope to prevent the predicted human catastrophe and create world peace with the urgency now required. All that follows will ensure that the happy, safe world we create is sustainable.

2. **The critical discovery**: Normal thinking is suddenly insane! The proliferation of WUD has suddenly made the innate *either/or* tribal way we all learn to think more deadly than cancer, AIDS, and the Black Plague—and more imminent than global warming, pollution, and depletion of resources. There is no cure, only prevention. Einstein's ANWOT solution offers the best means to prevent us from becoming the first species to deliberately create its own annihilation. We each will remain part of the problem until we awaken ourselves to the new reality: the proliferation of WUD has made the addictive tribal way of thinking, which has been adaptive for over a billion years, a terminal disease that is suddenly fatal to humanity. The next war will be the last. Our human brain, educated in ANWOT, focuses on our similarities rather than our differences and inspires win/win cooperation for mutual benefits.

3. **The newer Story of Us** upgrades "his" stories of male dominance, win/lose confrontation and tribal wars to a more accurate, scientifically verified "our" story featuring gender equality, cooperation for win/win outcomes, and sustained blissful peace. It identifies five stages of love and our mission as humane becomings, who are innately designed to direct our energy for the benefit of the greater system of which we are a part.

4. **The Genie Seminar** is a more effective interactive means of education that provides for lifetime learning and emotional support for everyone. This innovation will help ensure that our world is the happy and safe home we want and need.

5. **The Mental Freedom Control Panel** identifies the eight action choices available to our freed will. It enlightens us to the two choices that consistently bring what we want and the six that commonly are a source of difficulty.

6. **The Supreme Law of Cause and Effect** is the one law that all life and inanimate things must obey from the first day. Recent awareness of this law is the basis of our recent explosion of knowledge, the scientific method, and the growth of common sense. Other names for this law include the Supreme Law of Orderliness and Predictability, the Law of Truth, and the Law of the First Cause.

7. **The asymptote** is offered as our first symbol of oneness that, by the meaning we assign to it, releases sufficient energy to supersede the tribal patriotic, religious, and political symbols that divide our world into opposing either/or sides. Accurately verified by the scientific method, the asymptote

tells the updated Story of Us from the first cell to the present, thereby providing a trajectory that prepares us to anticipate our future.

8. **A word switch** is any symbol (i.e., word(s) or icon) that transforms and redirects the material-physical energy of the animal portion of our brain into the higher-level mental-spiritual intentions of our puzzle-solving human brain. Word switches provide us with a conceptual second signaling system to wisely *self*-manage our destiny. A glossary of word switches and new symbols is found on the EC websites.

9. **Strens,** a collection of proven wisdoms and success principles, enable our puzzle-solving genie organ to direct the power of knowledge to grant our wishes. The EC stren collection offers the proven wisdoms of giants who gladly shared their insights to wisely manage life's challenges. We are all born ignorant. Ignorance is a temporary condition. Collecting enough strens can make us mental-spiritual millionaires who create a joyous, fulfilling life even when fate and circumstance are unkind. *The Stren Book* is free at www.7plus2formula.org.

10. **The call to action** inspires the specific one-two-three action steps anyone can follow to popularize Einstein's solution. Anyone can become a mental-spiritual millionaire and enjoy a fulfilled life even when the world is unkind.

The ANWOT curriculum provides self-governance skills that free our wish-granting genie organ from animal-brain domination. Newer symbols and word switches transform us from high-level animals into humane becomings. The content includes the universal values that empower us to express the "high-test" moral-spiritual intentions embraced by the Golden Rule. The Genie Seminar inspires creative puzzle solving through the collective energy of group participants. Contrast this with the highest intentions of animal brain thinking, which support the authority of the tribal leader and tribal law, and ignore or punish creative thinking. The EC content is designed to provide our immature genie organ with the knowledge it needs to process information using common sense.

The EC curriculum contains new pieces of the puzzle that contribute to the higher-level function of our problem-solving genie organ.[24] Begin with the 7 plus 2 Formula to learn ANWOT and the love-creation skills that teach the Golden Rule. The seven essential mind-freeing, life-changing, world-saving word switches jump-start ANWOT,

---

[24] Links to EC web sites and books at www.peace.academy.

and the two still secret love-creation skills rapidly teach the Golden Rule. The thirty-day love-creation challenge will make the 7 plus 2 Formula automatic and effortless. As we acquire these pieces of the puzzle, we make ourselves mental-spiritual millionaires, expand our wisdom, and enjoy a wonderful world ... even when it doesn't treat us fairly.

ANWOT adds moral-spiritual values to the intentions of our animal brain. The Golden Rule embraces all those skills that elevate us to humane becomings. A single "each one, reach many" teacher of the 7 plus 2 Formula (you!) can initiate a domino effect that will circle the world. One million teachers is the estimated number required to influence our seven billion world citizens.

The three enjoyable, quick steps to becoming a teacher of ANWOT and the Golden Rule are readily accomplished:

1.   Learn the seven word switches and two secret love-creation skills.[25]
2.   Pay them forward to those in your reach with a click on your computer.
3.   When they thank you, ask them to do the same.

Regular practice for thirty days will make ANWOT and unconditional love creation automatic and effortless. Some may get it sooner, others a bit longer. The cost is zero, and the emotional rewards of offering the love skills that keep on giving will equal or surpass any other endeavor.

Civilization is sustained by moral-spiritual truths that embrace humane qualities: unconditional global love, forgiveness, gratitude, kindness, justice, compassion, empathy, humility, and cooperation and collaboration for mutual gain—all the qualities we strive for as humane becomings. As we acquire these skills, we make ourselves mental-spiritual millionaires, expand our wisdom, and enjoy a wonderful world. The EC content is forever *free* at its websites.

Benefits of the 7 plus 2 Formula

Consider the universal benefits:

1.   The scientific method to solve puzzles and prevent problems by common sense is added to the prewired solutions acquired through trial and error.
2.   Win/win cooperation for mutual gain becomes the effective means to resolve conflict.

---

[25] They are available on pages 65-74 and on the EC websites.

3. The problem-solving question "What will make things better for me and you (us and them) for now and the future?" replaces "What works for me and my tribe for here and now?" "My way is the only right way."

4. The Golden Rule (reciprocity) replaces "He who has the gold rules." "The love of power" becomes "the power of love."

5. We assume a creator role as humane becomings instead of remaining high-level animals. Each individual becomes his or her own person instead of remaining servant to our first programmers—instinct, tradition, and human dictators.

6. Becoming a mental-spiritual millionaire assumes a higher level of intention for love creation than becoming a physical-material millionaire. Good deeds and wise creeds are prized above greed and speed.

7. Our history as "his story" is updated to more accurately teach "our story." Feminine unconditional love energy is balanced with masculine muscular energy.

8. The future forecasting ability of our genie organ adds prevention to the trial-and-error learning that leads to war and cure.

9. Our species will survive and thrive in peace as we add commonsense problem solving through social intercourse and cooperative puzzle solving to the existing means to sustain the life cycle—sexual intercourse and harmful confrontation.

10. We solve the puzzle: "Why do we fill our world with fear, hate, scarcity, and war when we want happiness, unconditional love, abundance, and peace?"

Consider these personal benefits. You will:

1. Love yourself with the abundance that overflows to enrich your loved ones and humanity (a modern version of the Golden Rule).

2. Assume responsibility for your own happiness and love needs so you will welcome love from others rather than remain dependent on it.

3. Own the most powerful antidepressant. People who assume responsibility to love themselves sustain a high level of well-being.

4. Become your own lifelong friend and traveling companion 24-7.

5. Attain mental freedom and become your own person, no longer a slave to instinct and tradition, fate and circumstance, nature and your nurturers, and human dictators.

6. Know how to bully-proof your kids. When they learn to like themselves, they no longer will be overly sensitive to others' unkindness—and they won't become shooters.

7. Prevent problems instead of causing them. You will free your energy from blaming others or yourself (guilt) to use your best to do your best. Blaming is the most common way we create our own problems.

8. Make your life significant as an important force for world peace by becoming an "each one, reach many" teacher of love creation. Three simple steps require little time and energy, and cost nothing. Spreading love and kindness is one of the most satisfying things you will ever do.

9. Answer the universal questions: "Who am I?" and "What is my purpose?" You will live with chronic enthusiasm as you fulfill your mission as a humane becoming instead of a human being (i.e., a high-level animal).

10. Add the moral mental-spiritual intentions of your human brain that make your life meaningful to the mechanical material-physical intentions of your animal brain.

11. Become a mental-spiritual millionaire as you collect the wisdom that adds to true wealth. Mental-spiritual wealth millionaires consistently create a joyous, meaningful, fulfilled life experience even when the world doesn't cooperate; material-physical wealth millionaires are often depressed and even commit suicide.

What could provide more fun and fulfillment than consistently creating love in overflowing abundance to enrich your loved ones while you cocreate with others to make our world the home we wish and pray for? Please consider the likely consequences of ignoring the *biggest* puzzle and allowing our dominant *either/or* way of thinking to persist. United, we will start an unstoppable movement to popularize Einstein's solution to the *biggest* puzzle.

Call to Action

The essential task before us is converting what we know into constructive action. Mental-spiritual knowledge is humankind's newest source of power. It is more sophisticated and eloquent than material-physical power. Knowledge supported by commonsense wisdom enables us to fulfill our wishes and attain what we want and need. Misdirected knowledge makes us our worst enemy, which is now apparent with the proliferation of WUD. Knowledge provides the "aha" satisfaction of solving puzzles and granting wishes, but knowledge without action contributes nothing to humanity. The power of knowledge and wisdom unexpressed or misdirected is an inefficient use of energy.

ANWOT is Einstein's revelation of what we must do to solve the *biggest* puzzle. He devoted the last ten years of his life to advocating world peace. He told us what we need to do but not how to do it. We now know the cause of war, the cause of peace, and the need for education in ANWOT. Thanks to many creative individuals who discovered pieces of the puzzle and made them common knowledge, the EC has organized this new knowledge into a self-taught, one-stop location available to anyone and everyone, anywhere and everywhere, anytime and every time on our free websites. We now have both the knowledge and the means of free mass education to proceed to succeed. The EC curriculum offers a comprehensive collection of basic skills that teaches ANWOT.

We have all the ingredients we need except one: the will to act. Instinct and tradition resist change. Common sense is not common. Most individuals are reluctant to let go of established ways of thinking, even when they no longer make sense and have become dangerous. We are used to our long dependence on the power of authority and tradition that resists creativity. Our educational establishment is especially fixed in its ways, and those who hold power are reluctant to give it up. The innate herd instinct to remain loyal to a tribal leader has the powerful support of emotion. The pursuit of material-physical wealth, especially greed, is hardwired to reject new ways for the promise of a greater but intangible glory.

The EC randomly interviewed over two hundred individuals, asking if they wished or prayed for world peace.[26] The answer, yes, was all but unanimous. To the second question, "Do you do anything to bring about world peace?" most said nothing. They revealed their addiction to the helpless/hopeless attitude that one individual cannot make a difference. Some said that God or our president would have to solve the problem. However, most emphatically said yes to the question "Would you do something if you were provided an idea that made common sense?" A positive outcome of the growing primitive behaviors consistently in the news is that people worldwide are awakening to the urgent need for change. Our world citizens have never been so ready to take action. Imagine the power of unleashing our collective,

---

[26] See video file "Interviews.wmv" at www.anwot.org for samples of brief random interviews.

imprisoned, unconditional global love. ANWOT education is our best hope. Working together, we will be unstoppable. We *can* make a difference!

The ANWOT curriculum offers a commonsense scientific explanation of the cause of war, the cause of peace, and the specific content that teaches our highest intention: unconditional universal love. The Golden Rule is

- welcomed globally by religions, secular tribes, and spiritual gurus;
- enjoyable and easy to teach and learn by ordinary people requiring little effort;
- quickly effective with limited practice;
- free to anyone, anytime, everywhere on the EC websites;
- made rapidly viral through the domino effect; and
- timeless, evergreen, and universally wanted and needed.

Do you know of a better solution to sustainable peace that has these qualities? Pessimists say it is already too late to reverse the hands of the doomsday clock. But while changing the way we think can be more difficult than overcoming a food or drug addiction, it can be done. Working together, our collective energy will prevail.

Most effective thought leaders intuitively recognize the power of moral-spiritual Truth. We regularly hear advertisements to become material-physical millionaires to enhance one's personal lifestyle; few emphasize becoming mental-spiritual millionaires and world peace leaders. Motivational gurus offer wonderful programs on how to achieve "the good life" through making money, finding one's life companion, or achieving fame. They preach happiness, love, abundance, and peace of mind, but they have yet to teach the specific skills that put the Golden Rule into practice. They promise personal material-physical wealth for the students who can afford their services. Their higher intention commonly features the animal brain's priority, "He who has the gold rules."

The work needed for world peace is rarely addressed, and when it is, there is limited practical advice. Material-physical tribal might takes precedence over unconditional universal love. This is understandable because the worship of material-physical power is our most popular religion. When asked to indicate their net worth, most people will answer in dollars or "toys." Gandhi, Mother Teresa, Martin Luther King, Lincoln, and Jesus would hardly register. However, many gurus are beginning to include world peace on their wish list. They and other teachers of teachers are positioned to create rapid change—educators, corporate leaders, politicians, coaches, clergy, therapists, entertainment and sports personalities ... and ordinary individuals. The EC curriculum invites all people, anytime, everywhere to become love-creation teachers and popularize the 7 plus 2 Formula.

> *Never doubt that a small group of thoughtful, committed citizens*
> *can change the world. Indeed, it is the only thing that ever has.*
> *—Margaret Mead*

It worked for AA, Amway, Mary Kay, and every great religion. Now we must make it work for world peace.

CHAPTER 4

Discussion

In 1945, a scholar named Emory Reves published *The Anatomy of Peace*. Now almost forgotten, this book proposed the one answer to create permanent world peace. Einstein, Senator William Fulbright, Claude Pepper, Mortimer Adler, Thomas Mann, and many other luminaries endorsed it. Their open letter to the public was published in the *New York Times* and fifty other leading newspapers. It reiterated, "Peace by Law is what the people of the world, beginning with ourselves, can have if they want it. And now is the time to get it." The Associated Press also heralded the importance of *The Anatomy of Peace* in sixteen hundred newspapers. The book became a runaway best seller and was adopted as a textbook by Harvard, Yale, and Columbia Universities.[27]

Reves's proposal was quite simple. After debunking multiple alternative solutions for a sustainable world, he concluded that world law was the only way to prevent war. Sovereign nations would need to create a world court of universal law with the power to enforce compliance. Allegiance to the symbols of individual nations, religions, and political entities that separate us would have to submit to a higher law of orderliness. World law assumes the continuation of local allegiances: "New Yorkers are citizens of the city of New York and the state of New York and the United States of America. But they are also citizens of the world."

Reves became frustrated when he realized that nation-states were not about to give up their power to a global court of law, and he turned to other interests. Along with most of the world population, he had overlooked the fact that we already have a universal law that all life and inanimate matter, without exception, must obey. I am

---

[27] Emory Reeves, *The Anatomy of Peace* (Harper & Brothers, 1945).

referring to the Supreme Law of Cause and Effect (the Law). Other names designate attributes of this law: the Law of Orderliness and Predictability, the Law of the First Cause, the Law of Common Sense, the Law of Truth, and so on.

Emergence of the Scientific Method: Supreme Law of Cause and Effect

This law defines the orderly relationship of everything in the universe. It has done so since being set in motion by what has been called nature, God, the first cause, and various other names. Even the Ten Commandments, popularly accepted as the word of God, are consistently disobeyed through the gift of free will, but no one and no thing escapes the universal Supreme Law of Cause and Effect (i.e., the phenomenon of orderliness and predictability). All life and inanimate objects submit to this law, from the beginning of creation to the present, and we can predict with a high level of certainty that it will be so in the future.

The Law establishes the scientific method: Every effect has a cause. Every cause is the result of a prior effect, and so on. If we continue back far enough, we would reach the first cause or uncaused cause. The exact nature of the first cause remains an unsolved puzzle, although there are various hypotheses.

The supreme law that establishes Truth[28] and order in the universe does not have a physical presence. It exists as nonphysical conceptual reality, in mind and as spirit. Conceptual reality may be imagined by intelligent minds equipped with sophisticated symbols. Until the emergence of the human mind, no creature has had sufficient intelligence, imagination, intention, and *self*-consciousness to create and use sophisticated symbols to discover the Law. We are high-level animals, human beings in the process of discovering the Law to make ourselves humane becomings. Our long history of misguided actions can justifiably be forgiven because of our ignorance of the Law; we didn't know better. We are now discovering our highest intentions through an understanding of the Law.

A current and unfortunately popular false assumption pits science against spirituality and religion: "Science is antireligion!" The scientific method is not antagonistic to religion and spiritual truth. We are able to discover and intentionally direct the power of universal moral-spiritual Truth through the application of the scientific method. People of every religious and secular persuasion consistently and independently arrive at some version of the Golden Rule, universal unconditional

---

[28] Truth is conformity to fact, knowledge, actuality, reality, and fidelity to an original standard.

love, as the one standard to guide our thinking, feelings, and actions. Science now provides physical proof that confirms the role of spirituality. Darwin and others applied the scientific method to enlighten us that the driving force of evolution is reciprocity; individual cells, units, and organs (and now tribes) contribute to the larger system or face extinction. The cancer that takes and gives nothing in return kills its host and thereby makes itself extinct. We express the principle of reciprocity as the Golden Rule.

The scientific method is the application of imagination to awaken us to the need for raising conditional tribal love to the next level of sophistication: unconditional universal love. We can examine our slow awakening to the Supreme Law of Cause and Effect through eight critical marker events:

1. Several billion years ago, bisexual organisms divided into distinct genders and each developed specialized functions. Males of our species were assigned muscular might to protect the tribe, and the duty to spread twenty million sperm per day. Females were assigned nurturance power to protect progeny until they reached reproductive maturity, and the duty to attract a male to fertilize the one egg produced each month. Even though brains remained equal, males took advantage of their physical strength and aggressive nature to dominate.

2. Two million years ago, the brain, primarily the cortex, began to increase in size (350 percent, 400→1,400 gm.) and function, while other organs remained relatively the same. The emerging cortex is the center of imagination, *self*-consciousness, our second signaling system, creativity, and the freedom to become our own person.

3. Circa fifty thousand years ago, the human mind introduced a newer way of thinking by creating symbols. This added imagination to the animal brain's trial-and-error means of learning. Imagination is our means to create concepts and manipulate them to solve puzzles. The most significant innovation from the use of symbols was the emergence of conceptual *self*-identify (i.e., the addition of *self*-consciousness to consciousness). Symbols empower us with *self*-programming, *self*-mastery, *self*-initiation, and *self*-governance. The use of symbols, linking data by similarity, initiated our growing power to construct and to destroy.

4. Considerable time passed before the discovery of intentional universal unconditional love. The introduction of the Golden Rule in separate locations

about twenty-five hundred years ago is credited to a few males, Buddha and Jesus being among the most notable. This idea was radical and rebellious to the traditional animal brain's way of thinking: Might is right; my way is the only way.

5. The most dramatic initiation of change emerged circa three hundred years ago with the discovery and popularization of the scientific method. The awakening, rapid spread, and application of the Supreme Law of Cause and Effect, of orderliness and predictability, initiated an explosive growth of knowledge. The combination of masculine domination and the growing power of conceptual knowledge explains why history is "his" story, featuring "wars and whores."

    The globalization of the scientific method made possible rapid communication and travel, collection of accurate data, the presence of more scientists than in all of history, and a gigantic leap in the science of puzzle solving. Religions, secular tribes, and spiritual gurus who focused on conceptual values arrived at the same mental-spiritual values: reciprocity, civility, harmony, and the qualities that elevate us from high-level animals to humane becomings. The widespread awakening to the Golden Rule is the highest expression of the Supreme Law of Cause and Effect. However, the power of the Golden Rule has continued to be subject to the two-category *either/or* tribal thinking of the animal brain. Reciprocity only applies to members in good standing of the tribe.

6. One hundred and fifty years ago, Darwin and other scientists linked together pieces of newer conceptual knowledge to solve the puzzle of our origins. The discovery of evolution updated "his" story with a more accurate explanation of who we are and what we are about.

    At the same time, spiritual leaders, including the Jesuit priest Teilhard de Chardin, added a spiritual facet to the physical explanation of our evolutionary history. The new Story of Us and its creators were ignored, rejected, and punished as would be expected … until recent stirrings of interest.

7. On August 6 and 9, 1945, the scientific method led to the introduction of WUD. The proliferation of nuclear, biological, and chemical WUD to tribes that had already claimed the moral and religious right to use them "has changed everything except our way of thinking," as Einstein put it.

8.   This brings us to the "do or die" present. Our most knowledgeable world citizens tell us we are in a race between nirvana and Armageddon, and the finish line is within sight. Optimists say we have less than ten years to solve the puzzle; pessimists say it is already too late. Realists say we must try no matter the odds. After interviewing over 250 world experts, a high-level commission mandated by the United States Congress concluded in its report to President Obama that we should expect the use of WUD and we are losing the battle.[29]

The Supreme Law of Cause and Effect has been present since time immemorial and can reliably be expected to continue in the future. However, conscious awareness of the Law is emerging only recently through *self*-consciousness. Consciousness means "with knowledge." *Self*-consciousness means we are an entity with the power of knowledge. Science is enlightening the human mind to the universal orderliness established by the Law. We grow our creative and destructive power as we apply the scientific method to discover, record, share, and pass knowledge forward. Human selection is increasingly partnering with natural selection to determine our destiny, the fate of our loved ones, and all that is about us. The recent advances in technology and mass communication are creating an expansion of knowledge that exceeds our attainment of wisdom.

Self-enlightenment is the process of upgrading our symbols by adding meaning that accurately imagines the Law (universal wisdom, Truth). The meanings our ancestors assigned to symbols expressed what was true based on limited knowledge, superstition, and great leaps of faith that we now know contain inaccuracies. *Self*-consciousness is our means to awaken ourselves from our stupor and resonate with the one supreme law that connects us to the first cause.

Prevention is our only defense against WUD. Preventing the predicted human catastrophe cannot be accomplished by trial-and-error learning because the animal brain has limited conceptual awareness of the future. It is prewired by trial and error and tradition to manage issues favoring solutions that worked in the past. Preventing the predicted human catastrophe requires that we awaken and initiate the necessary commonsense ANWOT action that will make the predicted event a nonevent. Einstein's solution is quite doable. However, instinct and tradition that

---

[29] *World at Risk, The Report of the Commission on the Prevention of Weapons of Mass Destruction Proliferation and Terrorism.* Bob Graham, chairman. (Vintage Books, 2008).

promote addiction to *either/or* tribal thinking will be the biggest obstacles because the animal brain reacts to what is unfamiliar (i.e., innovation) with avoidance and physical aggression.

The animal brain views love *and* hate as love *or* hate, either/or. The common sense of our genie organ recognizes these conceptual qualities as both ... and. They are like the opposite sides of the *same* coin. Love and hate are abundant within each of us. When we love reciprocity, civility, wellness, education, happiness, philanthropy, abundance, and peace, we also simultaneously hate greed, savagery, disease, brainwashing, misery, selfishness, scarcity, and war. Love of greed, physical dominance, and bigotry can be destructive, while hate energy directed to such negative phenomena becomes a constructive force. Tribal love unbalanced by universal love explains our history of favoring war, confrontation, and punishment above peace, cooperation, and education to resolve differences and bring about the harmonious function of the interrelated tribes.

Senator William Fulbright's informed perspective is worth noting:

> So frequently it is pointed out that the human race has acquired the means of its own destruction that the shocking fact no longer shocks us. Everyone has heard it but no one takes it seriously; statesmen readily acknowledge the ability of the human race to destroy itself and then proceed to act as though it were not a fact at all. It is known but not believed, perhaps because it is impossible, or at least very difficult indeed, really to believe something that one has not seen or felt or touched or experienced.
>
> Most of what we learn, certainly in the field of politics, we learn by trial and error, which is to say, by going about our affairs in a customary way until by experience of error, we learn that the customary way is no longer workable and, accordingly, we revise it. It is a perfectly good way of learning as long as the error itself is not fatal or irreparably destructive. In matters of war and peace in the nuclear age, however, we cannot afford to learn by experience, because even a single error could be fatal to the human race. We have got to learn to prevent war without again experiencing it; we have got to change the traditional ways of statecraft without benefit of trial and error; and, in addition,

we have got to be right not just in most but in all of our judgments pertaining to all-out nuclear war.[30]

Humankind is on the brink of suicide. The use of chemical weapons in World War I and nuclear weapons in World War II serve as blaring alarms to wake us up. The forewarnings are many, and red alert sirens are increasing in volume. Many of our most informed citizens are telling us that we have been in a stupor, blindly following the directions of instinct and our nurturers. Stupidity (from the word *stupor*) is habitually doing what worked in the past when current knowledge is available to initiate better methods to deal with new challenges. This book intends to awaken us before the final act.

Hopelessness/helplessness has set in. Some believe we are already beyond the point of return. Optimists believe the united efforts of realists will be unstoppable. ANWOT requires learning the essential principles for success (strens), the process to teach it, and the will to proceed—*content, process,* and *will.* The EC provides the content and the process. The willpower must come from the collective energy of those sufficiently awakened to pass forward their gift to those in need. *Self*-consciousness of the Law enables us to replace stupidity with wisdom. Wisdom is applying common sense through conscious awareness of the Law. The urgency for ANWOT education is made clear as we upgrade "his" story to the newer "our" story.

The creation of language and symbols that accurately reflect the Law is our means to perfect our imagination; the more we awaken ourselves this way, the more we discover universal moral Truth. The discovery of conceptual reality, including sophisticated mental-spiritual consciousness, is directly linked to the human mind's growing awareness of the Law through the scientific method. This process has enabled religious and secular tribes to independently add conceptual Truth to material Truth. We now recognize that unconditional love and happiness are as essential as physical sustenance. We must learn to unconditionally love our *self* in such abundance that it overflows to enrich others. Love-creation teachers are necessary to spread the Golden Rule. We can't give away to others what we don't own! We must begin by recognizing the importance of liking our *self.* We all recognize that crawling leads to walking and then to running. Let's similarly recognize that liking our *self* is the first baby step to creating sufficient love that overflows to enrich

---

[30] Senator J. William Fulbright, preface to *Sanity and Survival,* by Jerome D. Frank (Random House, 1967).

the world. A dictionary definition of love includes "liking intensely." *Unconditional love* means "liking our self, grown up!"

Attention, Educators!

This book documents the need to upgrade the way we teach our citizens to think. Modern society prizes education, gives it high financial priority, and supports twelve years of formal schooling. We are emotionally committed to excellence, and we believe in what we do. Yet our methods are still expressive of the animal brain's intentions to thrive through win/lose competition.

Traditional education continues to teach allegiance to local values. History is taught as a series of wars and emphasizes the glory and victories of one's own tribe. Our education emphasizes the symbols that express the tribal intentions of our animal brain, rather than global symbols. It emphasizes win/lose competition for high grades and approval. We emphasize the animal brain's way of didactic learning as the "normal" expression of our unrecognized addiction to *either/or* thinking; it is the way teachers themselves learned to think. Education in unconditional global love, or the Golden Rule—the most important skill to create a civilized society—is limited, poorly taught, or prohibited. Emphasizing uncritical acceptance of authority inhibits creativity. The Genie Seminar inspires creativity and practical puzzle solving. Adding group participation through circles to the standard lecture format promotes social intercourse and skills in cooperative problem solving. The Genie group process can identify potential shooters and provide early intervention for mental issues.

The discovery through the scientific method of our creation through an evolutionary process leads to conclusions that modify the traditional assumptions established by our ancestors. It tells us we are highly evolved animals with the mental capacity to transform ourselves into humane becomings. We are beginning to intellectually accept the new story revealed by an understanding of evolution, but instinct and tradition refuse to yield to wisdom. The hardwired trial-and-error solutions remain the focus of how we educate people to think. "His" story according to the masculine perspective is still taught. Our future requires us to update our education, featuring a newer way of thinking. The obstacle to teaching ANWOT is not inability; it is the lack of will to trade tradition for commonsense creativity.

Those of us who are fortunate enough to be positioned to make a difference have the opportunity, responsibility, and mission to awaken the rest of our world citizens who cannot do it without assistance.

Solving the *Biggest* Puzzle

The solution to the *biggest* puzzle becomes apparent when we understand the relationship of the animal brain to our emerging human brain. The highest intention of our prewired animal brain is sustaining the life cycle through material-physical means, primarily sexual intercourse and tribal dominance. The highest intention of our intelligent, emerging genie organ adds sustaining the life cycle through moral-spiritual means, primarily social intercourse. Social intercourse is the civilized exchange of mental energy for the benefit of all participants. Our genie organ empowers us to elevate our species above the animals as it discovers and adds the power of moral-spiritual Truth to material-physical Truth. Moral-spiritual power is our means to transform ourselves from highly evolved animals into civilized humane becomings.

Civilization is a society of distinct entities contributing the products of their creative energy for the benefit of the whole. Civilization is marked by an advanced stage of development in the arts and sciences and by corresponding social, political, and cultural complexity. Our animal brain has succeeded in "civilizing" the cells and organs of our body so they all contribute their unique functions for the good of the whole. The challenge for our human mind is to civilize our diverse tribes. Civilization is sustained by moral-spiritual Truths that embrace the humane qualities of unconditional universal love, forgiveness, kindness, justice, compassion, and cooperation for mutual gain.

The animal brain has succeeded in establishing the wisdom of the body to survive in a savage society. Our human brain must now teach us the mental-spiritual Truths that create a civilized society. Our genie organ is discovering that the power of conceptual moral-spiritual values is superior to physical might. As we awaken to the universal power of moral-spiritual Truth, the Golden Rule becomes the destination, and physical power is one means, although not the best, to get there. Instinct, tradition, and human dictators resist giving up their power. Common sense will not be common until we teach ourselves ANWOT. We have the content and process to harness our energy for the good of the whole. We need only find a way to free our intelligent genie from control by our animal brain; then that energy will be unstoppable.

The *Biggest* Puzzle Summarized

The recent spread of the scientific method has made us godlike creators with the power to influence our own destiny and all that is about us. The discovery and proliferation of WUD has suddenly changed everything, except our way of thinking. The recent explosion of knowledge has initiated a race between nirvana and Armageddon, and the finish line is within sight. Our most informed citizens tell us we are about to become the first species to intentionally make ourselves history instead of continuing to make history. Pessimists give up! Optimists and realists tell us there is still time to prevent this catastrophe. Let's solve the *biggest* puzzle:

> *Why do we fill our world with fear, hate, scarcity, and war when we want and need HELP (happiness, enough, love, and peace)?*

We now know the cause of war is the way we think. It can be stated in one sentence: "My way is the only right way." The animal brain is limited in the use of imagination. It processes information into two categories, focusing on differences. *Either/or* thinking is the reason our language is dominated by patriotic, religious, and political tribal symbols that lead to harmful confrontation. Although once adaptive in the primitive environment of our ancestors, *either/or* thinking has become the silent disease that is about to slay us. We need not abandon our tribal symbols. We require only a universal symbol that enlightens us to the benefits of tribes cooperating for the greater good instead of competing to dominate.

The cause of peace can be summarized in one word: "reciprocity," more familiarly stated as the Golden Rule.[31] Einstein and others have told us what's needed to create sustained peace: "We shall require a newer way of thinking" (ANWOT). Our emerging human brain equips us with imagination. It solves puzzles by linking data according to likeness and chronology. The newer way of *both … and* thinking recognizes our origin from a single source, our connection to one another, and the benefits of cooperation for mutual gain above confrontation to assert dominance. The powers of imagination, intelligence, and initiation are our means to discover our two weapons with ultimate *constructive* power (WUC): common sense and the Golden Rule. We have yet to make common sense common; emotion usually prevails. We preach the Golden Rule but fail to effectively teach it. "He who has

---

[31] Modern versions of the Golden Rule are "Love my*self* with the abundance that overflows to enrich the world" and "What best works for my tribe and your tribe, for now and the future?"

the gold rules" presently outweighs the Golden Rule. Greed and speed will persist above wise creeds and good deeds until we create ANWOT and popularize the Golden Rule.

We now have the knowledge, the wisdom, and the means of communication to provide education in a newer way of thinking *free* to anyone and everyone, anywhere and everywhere, anytime and every time. The obstacle we have yet to overcome is our continued dependence on the instincts and traditions that have worked in the past. The introduction of imagination fifty thousand years ago marked the addition of conceptual might to physical might. Imagination uses symbols to solve puzzles. Wisdom is a newer source of mental might. As humankind discovers, shares, records, passes forward, and popularizes the scientific method, we expand our power of knowledge and wisdom exponentially. The concept of *self* adds *self*-consciousness to consciousness, *self*-programming, *self*-mastery, *self*-governance, creativity, and the power to partner with prior programmers to assume responsibility for our own destiny.

The popularization of the scientific method circa three hundred years ago marks the beginning of the exponential growth of knowledge. The newer story of our history updates "his" story to a newer "our" story, which tells us we are higher-level animals, static human beings that are uniquely equipped to make ourselves dynamic humane becomings. This new story reveals that the *either/or*, two-category way of thinking that was effective in a savage environment has suddenly become a fatal disease about to slay us. Our wisest citizens predict the likelihood of *self*-annihilation. However, our new story also awakens us to the actions we can take to prevent Armageddon and redirect our path to the blissful peace we want.

As we update our dominant "his" story with a more accurate "our" story, we may direct our creative energy from WUD to WUC. We can solve the *biggest* puzzle and prevent the human catastrophe that offers no second chance. The wonderful news is that we now have the means to transform insight into effective action.

The Educational Community websites offer what we believe is the first and only comprehensive curriculum that teaches Einstein's solution and is guaranteed forever free. They include powerful love-creation skills that teach the Golden Rule, a new vocabulary of word switches that free our intelligent genie from control by others to grant our wishes, a collection of one hundred strens (mental-strength-building wisdom) to become a mental-spiritual millionaire, a new universal symbol to turn on a newer way of thinking, the Mental Freedom Control Panel that identifies the eight choices available to our willpower, and essays that address more complex issues.

The EC's goal is to inspire one million love-creation teachers who will popularize Einstein's newer way of thinking through the domino effect.

The action required to solve the *biggest* puzzle is education in the skills that transfer the capital of our intentions from our animal brain to our intelligent *genie organ*. The EC's curriculum provides newer knowledge, verified by the scientific method that updates established beliefs to improve puzzle solving. The EC recommends the Genie Seminar as the preferred method to ensure continued progress in our emergence from high-level animals to humane becomings.

CHAPTER 5

A New Symbol to Convey the Essential Content of ANWOT Education

As a special feature of this book, Einstein's solution is presented here in "sound bite" fashion using the arrow (➔) for greater clarity in understanding the process of change. Think of each arrow as expressing a gradual *both ... and* progression from one extreme to the other with gradations in between, not as either/or when a horizontal division line or period emphasizes the separation between two extremes. New features are added to gradually modify old features rather than replace them. Thus, the process of emergence is more *both ... and* than *either/or*. Each gender has masculine and feminine hormones, just in different proportions. We commonly experience both love *and* hate toward the same person's behavior. New knowledge offers more accurate ways of thinking. However, we find established ways resist modification. *Either/or* thinking is the normal animal brain's way of thinking, which provides a false interpretation of actual reality. "His" story will slowly yield to new knowledge only if common sense is persistent and the 7 plus 2 Formula is paid forward to popularize ANWOT and the Golden Rule.

The emerging collection of assumptions, supported by the scientific method, falls into three categories: new knowledge, a newer way of thinking, and a newer way of learning.

1. **"His" Story of Us ➔ The New "Our" Story of Us:** Knowledge upgrades the accuracy of our established history and assumptive worldview. The new story reveals we are born from one source and connected to one another. It inspires action to elevate our intentions to cooperate for mutual benefit

instead of harmful confrontation to dominate others—to favor the power of love above the love of power.

2. **Animal Brain Thinking ➔ Human Brain Thinking:** Our upgraded story recognizes we are high-level animals (i.e., static human beings) in the process of evolving to dynamic humane becomings. Our human brain properly educated in ANWOT adds conceptual might to physical power.

3. **Dominant Didactic Education ➔ ANWOT Puzzle-Solving Education:** Education using the Genie Seminar is the tool to free our wish-granting genie from earlier masters to become our own person. ANWOT teaches reciprocity (i.e., the Golden Rule) to embrace mental-conceptual skills, such as unconditional love, forgiveness, kindness, justice, tolerance, compassion, and cooperation for mutual gain. ANWOT upgrades the animal way of thinking that demands allegiance to self, family, and tribe, and dominance over non–tribe members to embrace unconditional global love.

"His" Story of Us ➔ The New "Our" Story of Us

Survival and the well-being of our loved ones require that we update "his" story (history) to "our" story. The way we think, feel, and act is guided by the assumptions we make about our *self* and the world. New knowledge is awakening us to who we are and what we must do to survive and thrive. We are distinct from all other species by the gift of a new commonsense, puzzle-solving genie organ. Intelligence, imagination, and the ability to *self*-program our intentions bring with it responsibility and opportunity. We may use our new power of knowledge wisely to transcend ourselves into humane becomings, or stupidly to make ourselves the first species to intentionally *self*-annihilate, or anything in between. Our wisest citizens warn us that we have little time to prevent the worst expressions of our new weapons. *Self*-change begins with *self*-awareness! Our resistance to modify "his" story to "our" story has delayed our emergence from static human beings to dynamic humane becomings.

1. Life began six thousand years ago when God magically created everything in six days. ➔ Life on earth began 3.5 billion years ago as a single cell and is progressing to greater complexity and sophistication in an orderly cause-and-effect way.

2. God favors my tribe above others. He periodically, selectively, and magically intervenes to express His authority and have his way. ➔ The creative

force(s) applies the law of cause and effect (i.e., the law of orderliness and predictability) to all things living and inanimate. The human mind has been equipped with free will (*self*-programming) to assume responsibility for our destiny.

3. God favors males above females. Eve was created to serve Adam. ➜ The creative force provided both genders with equal intelligence but different roles in sustaining the life cycle.

4. God expresses his will through messages to specific males who then enforce the law. ➜ Humankind is distinguished from other life by the gift of imagination, creativity, and free will to become a partner in determining the destiny of our world.

5. History is "his" story according to the masculine perspective of domination by harmful confrontation (might makes right). ➜ The awakening to evolution creates a new "our" story in which humankind must add mental-spiritual might to cooperate for mutual benefit; reciprocity and the Golden Rule to surpass "He who has the gold rules."

6. Disobedience to God's (or human dictators') rule brings severe punishment, even damnation for eternity; obedience brings heavenly rewards. ➜ The supreme law for everything in the universe is orderliness: every effect has a cause, and every cause is the outcome of a prior effect. Humankind has a mission to live in harmony by making commonsense education common, and to prevent harmful behavior and self-annihilation.

7. Prayer: Begging, bargaining, and sacrificing are rewarded with special favors, including granting our wishes. ➜ Gratitude acknowledges that humankind has been given common sense, inspiration, and perspiration as powerful tools to grant our wishes.

8. Love is conditional for the benefit of self, family, or tribe; give to get. ➜ Love is unconditional; loving our self with the abundance that overflows to enrich the world is a complete, self-fulfilling act.

9. There is a master race (us) and subservient races (them). ➜ Creativity and power are shared for the good of the total community; there is no longer any "them."

10. Competing for scarce resources using physical might is "normal" and sane. ➜ Cooperation to grow, breed, and create new resources for mutual benefit is the sane means to survive and thrive.

11. Goal setting: Personal and tribal sense is supported by the authority of instinct and tradition, viz., "My way is the only way." ➔ Universal common sense is verified by the scientific method (i.e., cause and effect supports reciprocity as our highest intention).

12. Hero: The Rambo-type brave fighter brings glory to his tribe or has exceptional wealth and "toys." ➔ The ordinary person, often unglorified, contributes what he or she can offer to sustain blissful peace.

The discovery of symbols circa fifty thousand years ago was a marker event in history because it enabled us to solve puzzles through the power of imagination. This discovery was more important than the ability to stand erect or the discovery of fire or the wheel. The addition of conceptual power to physical power enabled us to construct and destroy, to love and hate, and to transform ourselves from human beings into humane becomings.

Another marker event was the discovery and popularization of the Supreme Law of Orderliness and Predictability, what we may also call the Supreme Law of Cause and Effect. Every effect has a cause, and every cause is the effect of a prior cause. Knowledge could be shared, recorded, passed forward, and applied to increase creativity. The exponential growth of the power of knowledge through imagination has made us rulers on earth with the free will to establish a blissful, peaceful home at one extreme, *self*-destruct at the other extreme, and anything in between.

Animal Brain Thinking ➔ Human Brain Thinking

The newer "our" story awakens us to our gradual evolution over 3.5 billion years from a single cell to multicellular organisms, to systems of specialized organs to create individuals with trillions of mutually supportive cells, families of individuals, and tribes of families. Sovereign tribes are now becoming interrelated to form a system of tribes. The new story reveals a creative impulse motivating us to higher levels of sophistication. Elevation to the next level succeeds when the component units work to support one another, each contributing its specialized function for the benefit of the whole. Lack of harmony leads to extinction.

The highest intention of the animal brain's operating system (i.e., its way of thinking) is to sustain the life cycle by sexual intercourse and to protect progeny to reproductive maturity. The new "our" story explains why we must update our way of thinking if we choose to continue to make history instead of making ourselves history. The new story makes apparent the need for education in the skills of social intercourse. We must transfer the capital of our intentions from our animal brain to our human genie organ.

1. Anatomy: Medulla, pons, pituitary, pineal body, cerebellum, thalamus; collectively the prehuman "animal" brain ➜ All these plus the cerebral cortex, our puzzle-solving genie organ.
2. Prewired with the best of the best action pathways proven to solve past challenges to survival ➜ Born a blank slate ready to be inscribed by various programmers; capable of learning *self*-programming, attaining *self-mastery* and *self-governance, becoming one's own person, and joining early programmers of the way we think, feel, and act.*
3. Sensory operating system (OS): Senses—seeing, tasting, touching, hearing, smelling—that focus on differences ➜ Imagination, which focuses on similarities and puzzle solving.
4. Motor OS: Primary signaling system composed of nerves, muscles, and chemical and electrical mediators, which are the final pathway to action. ➜ A nonphysical second signaling system is added, consisting of symbols linked to energy, trigger words, and word switches, and capable of influencing the primary physical sensory-motor system.
5. Automatic mindless regulation of the machinery of the body sustains the status quo and resists change. ➜ The genie-like ability to create nonphysical concepts can turn on the primary signaling system to initiate a physical action.
6. Absent or limited conceptual ability; sorts data according to superficial differences ➜ Applies conceptual skill (imagination) to recognize similarities; "sees" deep and wide, near and far, past and future.
7. *Either/or* thinking, "My way is the right way" for individual, family, or tribe ➜ Addition of *both ... and* thinking to promote well-being of interrelated community (i.e., humanity).
8. Win/lose competition dominates; lose/lose with WUD ➜ Win/win by cooperative problem solving for shared benefits.
9. Favors physical power; competes for scarce resources ➜ Applies creative puzzle-solving power to make wanted/needed scarce resources abundant.
10. Primary means to sustain the life cycle: sexual intercourse ➜ Addition of social intercourse, collective puzzle solving.

11. Learning by trial and error and tradition ➜ Addition of common sense verified by the scientific method.

12. Truth is one's personal sense based on authority. ➜ Truth is common sense verifiable by anyone and everyone, anytime and every time, anywhere and everywhere (i.e., the scientific method).

13. Private sense becomes personal truth. ➜ Addition of common sense to reveal universal truth.

14. What can I take for me, my family, and my tribe? ➜ What can I give to benefit the system of which I am a part for the good of all?

15. When the world no longer cooperates to satisfy our needs, frustration leads to blaming (the fight instinct) or avoidance (the flight instinct). ➜ Blaming and avoidance in response to perceived unfairness is understood as animal behavior to be managed through education and setting limits.

16. Escalation to attain dominance; "an eye for an eye, a tooth for a tooth" ➜ De-escalation to attain civilization and blissful peace; barter for truce.

17. CEO of action: instinct and tradition ➜ New CEO of action: imagination applying commonsense puzzle solving.

18. Attaining goals through conditional tribal love; indoctrination during formative years to support instinct and tribal traditions; domination by intimidation, fear, punishment, withholding physical or mental satisfaction, guilt ➜ Attaining goals through liberating education; unconditional global love embraces humane qualities of forgiveness, kindness, justice, compassion, cooperation, and gratitude; encouraging creativity, reinforcement of positive behavior.

19. Sustaining the life cycle: Emphasis on tribal survival by competition to win scarce resources—food, sex, money, titles, "toys," and so on. ➜ Emphasis on mental wealth for universal survival by cooperation and common sense to create abundant resources for all—unconditional universal love, forgiveness, kindness, justice, compassion, cooperation, sharing, and the like.

20. Conflict resolution and problem solving: Physical might is right, survival of the physically fittest, harmful confrontation, war ➜ Mental-spiritual might is right and superior to physical might; blissful peace.

21. Dealing with arousal energy (i.e., strain—the response to stress)
    a. Interpreted as "anger" ➜ energy is directed to confrontation ("fight" part of fight/flight instinct); harmful action

    b. Interpreted as "fear/anxiety" ➔ energy is directed to withdrawal, avoidance ("flight" part of fight/flight instinct)

    c. Interpreted as a "signal to take commonsense action" ➔ energy is directed to cooperative puzzle-solving action to restore peace; enlightenment to prevent harmful reaction

22. Managing deviance: Demanding compliance by punishing the deviant ➔ Self-examination to find the weakness in establishment education, then reeducating the deviant; limit-setting as needed to protect society if deviance is dangerous.

23. Dealing with diversity: Support the master race, dominate non–tribe members and force them to serve the master tribe ➔ Tolerance; encourage, support, and welcome whatever contribution each tribe can offer to the well-being of the global community.

Dominant Didactic Education ➔ ANWOT Puzzle-Solving Education

Education in ANWOT is the payoff action step. Enlightenment without action provides a brief personal "aha!" moment but no benefit to the well-being of our loved ones. ANWOT elevates the capital of our intentions from our animal brain to our human brain to recognize the superior benefits of mental-spiritual might. Education in the power of unconditional love adds eloquence to material-physical strength. We already have the knowledge and technology to proceed to succeed. The EC offers a comprehensive, commonsense ANWOT curriculum, perhaps the first. The challenge we face can be simply stated:

Do we have the courage to question tradition and the will to implement commonsense answers?

The collective energy of ordinary individuals will initiate an unstoppable movement.

1. Didactic education includes indoctrination (brainwashing) during our formative years to have allegiance to tribal values ➔ The addition of education in global allegiance will bring harmony and civilization to the total system.

2. Education through lectures and memorization ➔ Addition of the Genie Seminar as a newer, more creative process of education.

3. Teaches what to think and what is local "truth" (tribal law) ➔ Teaches how to think and how to discover universal Truth (The Supreme Law).

4. Teaches animal-brain language and values ➔ Teaches practical puzzle-solving skills.

5. Emphasizes dependence and obedience to authority ➔ Emphasizes mental freedom and *self*-governance through *self*-programming.

6. Favors trigger words that convey preprogrammed responses and tradition ➔ Favors word switches that invite creative thinking to address practical puzzles whose solutions provide global benefits.

7. We require nurturance during our formative years, and we believe we are entitled to keep receiving it. ➔ Our prolonged formative years provide the opportunity to learn *self*-programming, *self*-governance, *self*-mastery, and personal responsibility.

8. Behavior is determined by trial-and-error learning (instinct) and tradition ➔ Addition of commonsense, creative puzzle solving (i.e., the scientific method).

9. Teaches conditional tribal love, emphasizing patriotic, religious, and political symbols ➔ In addition, teaches unconditional *self*-love in abundance that overflows to enrich the world; teaches and emphasizes global symbols.

10. Education for tribal intentions ➔ Education for the benefit of humanity, civilization of our interrelated system.

11. Teaches dependence on authority ➔ Teaches us to become our own person; mental freedom.

12. Education's goal is to become a material-physical millionaire ➔ Adds the higher priority to become a mental-spiritual millionaire.

13. Tolerance for creativity: Ignore or punish creative thought that's not supportive of tribal law ➔ Encourage creativity in the arts and sciences, and verify its merits by the scientific method (common sense).

14. Power: Direct energy to increase physical might so the individual, family, and tribe can dominate non–tribe members; win/lose ➔ Direct collective energy to expand mental-spiritual might for the benefit of humanity; win/win.

15. Process: Tribal information is absolute and must be accepted and respected. ➔ The Genie Seminar encourages collective creativity through group

discussion; all teaching is transparent, subject to question and verification by common sense.

16. The teacher is an authority figure, commanding the student to learn by rote and repetition. ➜ The teacher is a facilitator and motivator who introduces content and encourages group creativity; discussion focuses on the practical application of content.

17. Tribal values outweigh universal values. ➜ Universal values outweigh tribal values.

18. Content is biased toward a traditional "his" story. ➜ Content emphasizes the new "our" story, transformation into humane becomings, ANWOT, and progressing from dependency to personal responsibility.

19. *Either/or* thinking emphasizes right/wrong differences, superiority of my tribe's way, and us vs. them. ➜ *Both ... and* thinking emphasizes similarities, tolerance for diversity; all tribes are "us," and "them" disappears.

20. Reinforcement and approval are based on performance on academic tests, pass/fail competition. ➜ Endorsement is based on doing one's reasonable best, according to the individual's skill level; cooperation for mutual benefit and civility; emphasis on anti-bullying, detection, and early intervention that prevents harmful aggression; failure to thrive is usually the inadequacy of the system rather than that of the student.

21. Anger management, stress management, and relaxation skills are ignored or avoided. ➜ These skills are a standard part of the curriculum.

22. Focus is on teaching students up to the age of eighteen when the brain is most malleable and receptive to brainwashing. ➜ The addition of lifelong education when the brain attains the maturity and mental strength to become one's own person. The Genie Seminar is an ideal means to accomplish this.

23. Traditional content emphasizes our differences and competition as the way to resolve conflict. ➜ The emphasis is on tolerance for diversity, conflict resolution skills, and peacemaking.

24. Emphasis is on reading, writing, arithmetic, and making a living. ➜ The addition of generic spiritual values and social intercourse (how to live in harmony); unconditional universal love, forgiveness, kindness, justice, cooperation, and values that transform us from high-level animals into humane becomings.

The Educational Community's comprehensive ANWOT curriculum is designed to rapidly popularize Einstein's solution to the most important puzzle:

Why do we fill our world with fear, hate, scarcity, and war when we want and need HELP (happiness, enough, love, and peace?

The EC's ANWOT curriculum is our gift to you forever free:

www.peace.academy: The starting point with links to other EC websites

www.worldpeace.academy: Informative videos

www.7plus2formula.org

    a) The 7 plus 2 Formula in script, audio, and video
    b) Book 1: *World Peace in Three Years or Less ... or Else!*
    c) Book 2: *The 7 plus 2 Formula*
    d) Book 3: *The Stren Collection*

www.EinsteinsSolution.org: The skills to become a love-creation teacher

www.lovingmenow.org: The basic skills of the 7 plus 2 Formula

www.anwot.org: Einstein's solution. A Newer Way of Thinking (equivalent to a three-credit college course)

CHAPTER 6

The 7 Plus 2 Formula

The newer way of *both ... and* thinking education in ANWOT becomes available as we attain physical maturity and learn the skills that create happiness, unconditional love, abundance, and sustainable peace.

7 Mind-Freeing, Life-Changing, World-Saving Word Switches

Easy-to-learn skills empower us to elevate ourselves from the intentions of our mechanical-physical animal brain to those of our mental-spiritual human brain so we can assume responsibility for our destinies. A mere seven mind-freeing, life-changing, world-saving word switches listed below can accomplish this! These effective word switches empower us to take control of our well-being.

1. Substitute "I think I can," the spark of energy that inspires action, for helpless/ hopeless trigger words like "I can't," "Why bother," "It's too hard," "What's the use," "To hell with it," and "Ferk it."
2. Substitute the personal responsibility word switch "I allow" for the blaming words that express dependency and cause war, "He (she, they, it, the world) makes me ..."
3. Substitute "I could" for the dictator phrase "You should." Consider alternative choices.
4. Most importantly, substitute "both ... and," a phrase that focuses on similarities, for the trigger word "either/or" that divides the world into opposing categories and promotes bigotry, prejudice, and intolerance.
5. Regularly substitute the puzzle-solving sentence "What is most likely to make things better for me *and* you (my tribe *and* your tribe) for now *and*

the future?" for "What makes things better for me and my family (my tribe) for here and now?" or "My way is the only way."

6. Substitute "energy" for "anger," "fear," and "anxiety." Energy turns on puzzle solving while anger, fear, and anxiety turn on the fight/flight response.

7. Substitute "urgent" for "emergency" and immediately assign high, medium, or low priority to the urgent situation. Instinct biases us to interpret low and medium priority issues as emergencies, causing a harmful overreaction.

Here is how you will benefit from each of these word switches: "Yes, I think I can" turns on the energy we need to get results. Word switches two, three, and four free our thinking from mental slavery to the instinct and traditions that nature and our nurturers program into us while we are helpless and immature, and it is appropriate for us to blindly obey. The universal problem-solving sentence is the magical tool that, regularly used, creates commonsense solutions that work while harmful alternative actions wither away from disuse. Word switches six and seven diminish the formerly effective instinctive anger and the emergency fight-or-flight impulsive responses that are least likely to work in today's world and that often get us into trouble. Group mental puzzle solving offers preferred solutions.

***

This brings us to the 2 in the 7 plus 2 Formula—the two most powerful yet still relatively secret universal love-creation skills that teach the Golden Rule … unconditional love creation with the abundance that overflows to enrich the world.

1. **Emotional *self*-endorsement**
2. **The reasonable best measure of *self*-worth**

These two skills, regularly practiced for thirty days, more or less, can be made automatic and effortless. If we only popularize the 7 plus 2 Formula, ANWOT and the Golden Rule, these universal skills will achieve most of our mission. To learn more, visit the EC websites, especially www.peace.academy and www.worldpeace.academy.

Every life form contains an energy-producing factory. Love is the direction of energy for the benefit of someone (including our self) or something. For us to survive and elevate ourselves to higher spiritual levels, we must teach ourselves to love unconditionally with the abundance that overflows to enrich the world. Until we learn to provide our own minimum daily requirement (MDR) of happiness and love, we will remain addicted to someone or something beyond our control to sustain our well-being. The *self*-affirmation skills we require to assume personal responsibility for happiness and unconditional love are discouraged by contemporary society. Let's get started by making the two secret love-creation skills common knowledge!

Secret Love Creation Skill #1: Emotional *Self*-Endorsement

Few people know how to emotionally endorse themselves. Can you imagine being able to teach yourself to create good feelings with the same ease that you naturally feel guilty, embarrassed, ashamed, or depressed? You can ... if you learn how to endorse your *self* emotionally and practice doing so. *Self*-endorsement is the secret to love creation.

During our tender, malleable years, we lack the equipment to emotionally endorse ourselves. Survival requires others to provide the love and approval we need. Our educational system not only does not routinely teach us to direct love energy to ourselves, but it also tells us we are self-centered, egotistical, and wrong to do so. Approval, recognition, love, and support from others are worth working for. But when we take responsibility for our own emotional MDRs, what we get from others becomes a bonus, rather than a necessity. When you're less needy, it is easier to be a lover than a love junkie.

Good feelings stir us to continued action. Immediate satisfaction is critical to sustain the work and practice required to attain the rewards of virtually every important skill. Knowing we are doing something worthwhile is intellectual endorsement; its satisfaction is usually weaker than emotional joy. Emotional endorsement is the immediate satisfaction that allows us to enjoy the work we do now in order to attain more satisfaction later.

Here's the wonderful news: We are already well practiced in emotionally directing love energy. We stomp our feet and yell with abandon at sports events, applaud and cheer a musical performance, and know how to get that baby to smile and the dog to wag its tail. We even express our enthusiastic approval to food: "Wow!" to that chocolate ice cream sundae. The skill is there! We simply need to direct emotional endorsement to our *self*.

Take time each day to provide for both your physical and your emotional well-being. After you exercise, or while you're eating breakfast, take a few moments to consider your emotional MDRs. You can give yourself MDRs anytime and anyplace, but if you become accustomed to doing so at certain times of the day, you will form the habit quickly. Make a short, positive statement to yourself, such as "Atta girl/boy!" Or use detailed imagery to create a self-endorsement fantasy.

Would you like to turbocharge your emotional self-endorsement skills? Apply "secondary endorsement." Secondary endorsement is endorsing yourself each time you engage in the very worthy act of emotionally endorsing yourself. Like forging through a jungle, unless it's regularly maintained, the new path will soon be overgrown until not even a trace remains. Neglecting your emotional needs causes self-put-downs to reappear and overpower the new habits. Secondary endorsement is the maintenance that keeps the path of self-endorsement clear.

"Hurrah! Congratulations to me for endorsing myself. That's worthy of a special bonus. I deserve to endorse myself for endorsing myself."

Behavior that is rewarded is repeated! With practice, secondary endorsement will become automatic and effortless. Give yourself credit each time you endorse yourself. You will be pleasantly surprised to discover that secondary endorsement will rapidly build mental muscles that you will be proud to own.

Pull-ups (i.e., self-endorsements) serve you better than put-downs. When you endorse yourself for endorsing yourself, you pull yourself up and keep yourself up. Become consciously aware of any endorsement you initiate. As soon as you recognize that you're endorsing yourself, enthusiastically call forth images such as blinking lights, musical accolades, and cheers as your signal to automatically trigger the secondary endorsement you deserve for endorsing yourself.

As you begin to feel consistently good about yourself, you'll notice that people will enjoy being with you and seek out your company more often. People are attracted to someone with an upbeat attitude. The friends and popularity everyone desires are far more likely to develop when you no longer need others to reassure you that you're okay. And you can add your new, upbeat attitude to your list of emotional MDRs.

Here is a special bonus. As you create the MDR of loving-my-self pull-ups, you will attain the highest expression of unconditional love: forgiveness. Forgiveness = for + giving. The hardest form of love is forgiving one who has or is perceived to have done harm to us. Remember the most powerful words ever spoken: "Forgive them; they know not what they do." Begin with *self*-forgiveness.

Secret Love Creation Skill #2: The Reasonable Best Measure of Self-Worth

Most people evaluate their self-worth by the outcome of what they do. The RB (reasonable best) test is an "input" measure. It emphasizes your efforts, not the results of your efforts.

This skill would be simple if we were not so strongly indoctrinated not to practice it. In any situation, simply recognize when you're doing your reasonable best and endorse yourself for doing so. You will create and maintain positive feelings about yourself no matter what you are trying to achieve. You can only control your input into a situation. The outcome is usually influenced by many factors that you can do little or nothing about, so it's unrealistic to expect that you can control it. Yet most people have been taught since childhood to regulate their feelings about themselves by focusing on the outcome.

Do you still depend on the outcome of your efforts as the primary measure of your self-worth? Consider these outcome measures that create a positive or negative emotional response:

I'm OK if:
he/she loves me
I won
my efforts worked out
they accept me
I got an A
my salary is increased
the audience applauds
you understand
they think I'm attractive
I own a _____
the kids do well
I didn't make a mistake

You're utilizing healthy, realistic criteria to create positive feelings about yourself whenever you answer yes to this question: "Am I doing my reasonable best?" Even if you don't attain the outcome you desire!

But isn't it natural to feel bad when things don't work out?

Of course! It's normal to experience hurt when things don't work out the way you would have liked, or when you've been treated unfairly. But applying the RB test balances your pain or disappointment. By creating a sustained level of positive feelings about your *self*, you can manage your discomfort while working to resolve it.

How do I know what my reasonable best is?

Your reasonable best is the best you can do in a situation, considering your resources. Your intelligence and knowledge is less than perfect. You have time restrictions and commitments to many obligations. If you're in doubt about what your reasonable best is, work with someone else to help set realistic goals.

Suppose I'm not doing my reasonable best. Don't I deserve to feel bad?

Certainly not! Improvement requires practice and patience; setbacks are to be expected along the way. Each time you recognize you aren't doing your reasonable best, you create an opportunity to improve until you reach the level of your reasonable best. Your appropriate response is to say:

> I didn't do my reasonable best, but I'm recognizing the fact that I could be doing better. Only by recognizing an imperfection can I take the positive step of calling forth more effort and teaching my*self* to do better. I deserve to feel good for facing this shortcoming.

Most people beat on themselves when they discover they aren't the way they should be. Such *self*-put-downs lead to avoiding facing faults. Becoming aware of shortcomings, imperfections, or mistakes *is* your reasonable best! The reasonable best measure prepares you to apply problem solving and learn from your mistakes.

Putting our *self* down because we are less than perfect, less than we want to be, is a negative response that wastes our valuable energy without correcting the situation. The mistakes we make or our occasional poor judgment will probably lead to unpleasant consequences. Why pay twice by attacking our *self*-worth? Would you pay for your groceries and then get back in line to pay again ... and again?

Make the RB test a habit by asking frequently throughout the day, "Am I doing what I reasonably can?" If the answer is yes, immediate, enthusiastic self-endorsement is in order. If the answer is no, congratulate yourself for finding an opportunity to improve your efforts. Whether the answer is *yes* or *no*, you will have created a win-win situation for growth and *self*-worth.

Emotional Self-Endorsement: A Case Study

This case study illustrates our MDR for approval. It helps you to understand the power of these two love-creation skills. Most people are aware of the term "minimum daily requirement" because we see it on food and vitamin labels: "One serving has 50% of the minimum daily requirement of vitamin C." Just as our body has minimum daily physical requirements, we require a minimum daily dose of emotional satisfaction to sustain our mental vigor. Today, we are very aware of our physical need for food, vitamins, warmth, sunshine, and so on, and we know where and how to get them. Few of us, however, recognize that we have a minimum daily requirement for approval and love to sustain us. Are you such a person?

Caroline was having an especially difficult day. Before she left for work, her husband complained that she never showed any interest in his career. At the office her boss rejected the proposal she'd put extra effort into, and her secretary quit, telling her she was impossible to work for. Caroline sat at her desk, took a deep breath, and closed her eyes. She pictured herself marching down Main Street, the VIP in a parade. A brass band playing "The Most Beautiful Girl in the World" marched behind her. Two young women dressed in colorful costumes walked along in front of her, carrying a banner that stretched across the street. The banner read "Hurrah for Caroline!"

After a few minutes of engaging in her pick-me-up fantasy, Caroline returned to reality with renewed energy and enthusiasm. She took problem-solving actions. She put in a requisition for another secretary, phoned her husband to tell him she wanted to discuss his complaint, and began revising her proposal.

Six months ago, if Caroline had been confronted with only one of the circumstances she found herself in today, she would have dwelled on her shortcomings, mentally beat on herself, become depressed, and considered herself a failure. Now she is able to look at criticisms from others objectively, without putting herself down.

Caroline came to see me because of her recurring bouts of depression and a variety of physical complaints, including headaches, stomach queasiness, and insomnia. I soon discovered that Caroline's mental and emotional state was usually dependent on others' reactions to her. If people praised her or otherwise showed their approval, she felt good about herself and remained in a cheerful frame of mind. She seemed unable to cope with critical comments, however. Whether or not the criticisms were valid wasn't the issue. Because she didn't possess the skill

71

of cultivating self-esteem, Caroline reacted to the criticism with a depression that was often incapacitating, causing her to stay in bed or lie down with a headache.

Caroline was an intelligent young woman who was well informed about physical fitness and nutrition. It appeared to me that she pampered her flesh but neglected and even abused her mental well-being. She obtained at least the MDR of her physical needs, such as vitamins and minerals, so one day I asked her if she paid any attention to *emotional* MDRs.

"No." She smiled weakly. "I've never heard of such a thing."

"Could you imagine that just as your body has minimum needs for certain physical substances, your emotions also have daily requirements?"

"I'm not sure what you're getting at."

"I'm saying that you can feel better about yourself and suffer far less from depression by taking responsibility for giving yourself your MDRs of emotional nutrition."

"What do you mean by MDRs of emotional nutrition?"

"Your emotional MDR is the minimum daily requirement of positive feelings about yourself that you need each day to sustain your well-being."

"How can I give these MDRs to myself?"

"By substituting positive statements for the negative, demoralizing statements you usually make about yourself. Look in the mirror first thing in the morning and tell yourself, 'I'm lovable. I'm a hot sketch.' Or sing about your accomplishments while you're in the shower, or walk proud, as if you know you're somebody. Recognize and let go of self-pity, blaming, and what-if worrying; use your newfound energy to develop an attitude of gratitude. Assign yourself a unit every time you think or say something positive about yourself until you reach, let's say, at least ten a day. You can add up the units in a notebook or just do it mentally."

Caroline was skeptical, but she agreed to try what I suggested. Like many depressed individuals, at first she had difficulty thinking of anything positive to say about herself. With a bit of effort, however, she began to list some qualities that led her to believe that she was just as worthwhile as anyone else—for instance, that she was friendly, neat, and a hard worker. By focusing her attention on what she had, her accomplishments, and what she might attain, she had less time to put herself down. Her mood improved.

One day Caroline decided to jot down the units of approval she received from others. At the end of the day, her total was two. "If I depended on others for my emotional MDRs, I'd be depressed most of the time," she said.

Caroline, like most of us, was far too dependent on what others thought of her. She let her mood be controlled by people and events that were, predictably, unpredictable. It is appropriate for all of us, including Caroline, to depend on others for our emotional MDRs when we are children. Children don't have the mental resources to create their own feelings of self-worth. As adults, we don't have to react in the same way; indeed, we are unwise to remain so dependent.

We are encouraged to do more and more for ourselves as we continue to mature. We dress ourselves, take care of our personal needs, choose our lifestyle, and learn to support ourselves. In virtually every area of life, we are taught, and expected, to take care of ourselves, except where our emotional well-being is concerned.

Wouldn't you be insulted if, at this stage of your life, someone tried to brush your teeth for you or feed you? Yet not only are you not taught to provide for your emotional well-being, but you are even taught *not* to be kind to yourself. You are admonished if you say good things about yourself, especially if you share your self-satisfaction with others.

Larry, an engineer with an interest in technology, was pleased with the original software he'd created for his computer. He took a great deal of pride in showing it to his friends. One evening his mother took him aside and told him he was acting like a braggart. "She always told me that praise only counts if it comes from someone else. She says I'm selfish, vain, and an egotist if I say anything good about myself or what I've done."

Larry had worked hard at providing for his emotional MDRs. His tech ability was near the top of his list. Larry's mother didn't recognize that he was simply attempting to share his accomplishments with others, not lord it over them.

We are so strongly taught not to provide for our emotional MDRs that most people find it very difficult to do so. We understand that it's healthy to use our energy for *self*-encouragement rather than *self*-blame. Yet the lifelong repetition of *self*-put-downs, such as "I'm stupid," "I'm a jerk," or "I should've known," are so ingrained and so natural that making positive statements about our *self* feels awkward. Don't become discouraged if you don't get immediate results with your emotional MDRs. Think of the units of self-put-downs you've been giving yourself daily. With lots of practice, just as you would gradually strengthen a muscle, the positive statements can catch up with, challenge, and overtake your habitual, negative mental put-downs.

Just as we don't know the exact number of vitamins, minerals, amino acids, and other nutrients we need to enjoy optimum physical health, we don't know the exact number of MDRs we need to satisfy our emotional well-being. As we increasingly create more emotional MDRs, however, we'll sustain our well-being more confidently. As you experiment with this idea, you'll discover the number of MDRs you need to give you fuel to carry you through the day. Ten units was Caroline's starting point. You can also start with ten and increase the amount up to twenty, thirty, or as many more units daily as you need. You'll know that you have created sufficient MDRs when you're able to maintain your well-being on a consistent basis and face life's challenges, energetically and enthusiastically.

APPENDIX A

Five Essential Ingredients to Succeed in Any Endeavor

Like the flour, water, yeast, and salt needed to make bread, there are five raw materials required to develop *self*-mastery, to survive and thrive: faith, work, patience, direction, and risk taking. And they are available to everyone. Money, unusual intelligence, connections, good health, and magic are not needed.

1. **Faith:** Believe that "I can make a difference." Without faith in our power, we won't try. We generate energy for our first step when we say, "Yes, I think I can. I will!"
2. **Work:** Inspiration follows perspiration. Preparation and the practice required to succeed in our endeavors can be very satisfying.
3. **Patience**: The benefits of most worthwhile skills are not realized immediately. Patience is acquired through emotional *self*-endorsement.
4. **Direction:** We may stand on the shoulders of those giants who have preceded us who gladly share their wisdom so that we may avoid their mistakes.
5. **Risk-taking:** Acquiring new ways usually means letting go, even "murder," of established behaviors (never people) that no longer work and have become dangerous.

APPENDIX B

The Asymptote: Our First Universal Symbol of Oneness

We have yet to create a single symbol of our universal humanity that calls forth the same emotional power as the patriotic, religious, and political tribal symbols in our current language, including flags, the Muslim crescent, Christian cross, the Jewish six-pointed star, and the Nazi swastika.

If we plot the significant events of our evolutionary history on a chart, they form an *asymptote*. An asymptote is a line that curves as it progresses toward an end point without ever touching it. Touching the end point represents "the end of the line." The asymptote is an ideal symbol to express our origin from a single source. It illustrates the sudden, rapid change in the growth of power, causing the need for urgent, collective, problem-solving action to prevent the foreseeable disaster (i.e., reaching the end of the line). The asymptote can serve as our first universal symbol to call forth our new story with greater passion than tribal symbols.

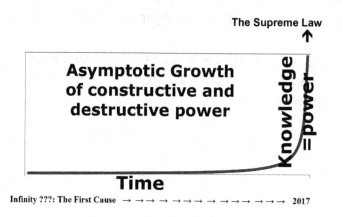

The Supreme Law

Asymptotic Growth of constructive and destructive power

Knowledge = power

Time

Infinity ???: The First Cause → → → → → → → → → → → → → → → 2017

Critical Events in the Timetable of Creation
Upgrading "his" story to "our" story

1. **Three and a half billion years ago**: Single cell evolves into complex individuals with fifty trillion cells and multiple organs, coordinated by animal brain.

2. **Billions of years ago**: Organisms are divided into two genders, each with specialized features to ensure survival of progeny and species.

3. **A billion years (?) ago**: Consciousness emerges, *either/or* thinking!

4. **Two million years ago:** The human brain progressively enlarges 350 percent while other organs remain relatively the same, increasing intelligence.

5. **Fifty thousand years ago:** The introduction of tribal symbols fosters imagination, an increase in creativity, and the discovery of conceptual reality; *self*-consciousness and *self*-programming (free will) are added to consciousness; spiritual might (conditional tribal love) is added to physical might; and imagination functions as a puzzle-solving, wish-granting genie.

6. **Twenty-five hundred years ago:** Unconditional universal love is introduced to conditional tribal love (Buddha, Confucius, Krishna, Jesus, others); *both ... and* thinking is added to *either/or* thinking; and the power of universal love is added to the love of tribal power.

7. **Three hundred years ago:** The spread of the scientific method leads to the exponential growth of knowledge, and communication technology hastens the verification of knowledge by anyone and everyone, anywhere and everywhere, anytime and every time (i.e., common sense).

8. **One hundred fifty years ago:** The puzzle of our origin is solved as evolution is verified by the scientific method, and the significance of the newer story of our creation is resisted by the established "his" story. More scientists are alive today than throughout all of history.

9. **Seventy-five years ago:** The introduction and proliferation of WUD offer no second chance.

10. **Present:** "Do or die" race between Armageddon and nirvana is in progress. We teach ANWOT to elevate our species from human beings (high-level animals) to humane becomings, thereby preventing *self*-annihilation or some lesser degree of human catastrophe.

APPENDIX C

The Mental Freedom Control Panel (MFCP)

The MFCP identifies eight choices available to us when we free our will from instinct and tradition (i.e., become our own person). Puzzle solving and *self*-endorsement, actions four and five, work with uncanny effectiveness to consistently attain desired outcomes; they get rid of blame and guilt. The other six commonly bring what we don't want. With a little practice, we can teach ourselves to recognize these alternative choices. We create a wonderful life when we regularly make the two wise choices and avoid those that usually create problems.

1. **Blaming-out:** mentally attacking another.
2. **Blaming-in** and **secondary blaming:** mentally attacking our self (guilt, put-downs).
3. **Avoidance:** mentally running from a stressful situation. This includes procrastination, substance abuse, excuses, dropping out, and the like.
4. **Puzzle solving:** the "magical" sentence—what is most likely to benefit me and you (my tribe and your tribe) for now and in the future?
5. *Self*-**endorsement** and **secondary endorsement:** unconditional love creation—"Atta boy!/Atta girl!" "I deserve to be proud."
6. **Helplessness/hopelessness (the H/H response):** the devastating give-up "Why bother?" response that shuts down our energy factory.
7. **What-if worry response:** wasting energy by exaggerating negative alternatives while neglecting the positive and most likely outcomes. Anticipating the worst leads to inappropriate anxiety and phobias.

8. **Mind/body response:** mind-over-matter reactions, such as tension leading to headache, back, or muscle pain, and harmful changes to our physiology, the machinery of our body.

The first three actions are primitive symbolic expressions of our physical fight-or-flight instinct. Puzzle solving (action four) applies common sense to create win/win outcomes for all parties, present and future. This one sentence could change our world if we teach enough people to practice it. There is no emphasis on blaming. Energy is not wasted on resentment, avoidance, and other nonproductive actions. While not actually magic, the results will often seem magical. Self-endorsement (action five) creates the unconditional love for our self and others that frees us to welcome love from others instead of remaining dependent on it. The hopeless/helpless response (action six) is the most devastating because it turns off problem-solving action. "What-iffing" the *worst* outcome rather than the *best* or *most likely* outcome (action seven) is carried over from our ancestors' need for constant vigilance in a life-threatening environment. The influence of mental stress on our physical state (action eight) is becoming increasingly apparent.

"Secondary blaming" (action two) is blaming our self for blaming our self. "Secondary endorsement" (action five) is endorsing our self for endorsing our self. Even after people learn that self-blame for mistakes is not productive, they commonly find they continue to do so and then make things worse by attacking themselves: "I'm such a jerk, I should have learned by now." On the other hand, few individuals recognize that if *self*-endorsement is one of our most positive actions; we should endorse our self when we endorse our self, thereby strengthening our positive action.

Note: These eight mental response patterns are rarely either/or. They are intertwined, one response often stimulating another. These combinations result in an infinite variety of patterns, forming a characteristic *personality print* akin to a fingerprint. We do well to emphasize puzzle solving and self-endorsement and attack our negative mental responses, *not* ourselves! To learn more, visit the EC websites: www.peace.academy; www.worldpeace.academy; and www.lovingmenow.org.

APPENDIX D

Become a Mental-Spiritual Millionaire: Further Reading

The first two books are forever *free* at www.7plus2formula.org:

1. Donald Pet, MD, *The 7 plus 2 Formula* ➔ *Happiness, Love, and Peace.* Expands the concepts in this book.
2. Donald Pet, MD, *The Stren Collection.* The commonsense wisdoms of thought leaders that make life wonderful.
3. Jerome D. Frank, MD PhD, *Sanity and Survival, Psychological Aspects of War and Peace* (Random House, 1967)
4. Jerome D. Frank, MD PhD, Persuasion and Healing, A Comprehensive Study of Psychotherapy (Schocken Books, 1963, 1974).
5. Jack Canfield, *The Success Principles* (Harper Collins, 2005, 2015). Sixty seven Success Principles to get from where you are to where you want to be.
6. Brock Chisholm, *Can People Learn to Learn? how to know each other* (Harper & Brothers, 1958). What we must learn to deal with modern existence.
7. Emery Reves, *The Anatomy of Peace* (Harper & Brothers, 1945). Rational thinking about world peace endorsed by Albert Einstein and leading luminaries of the time.
8. Kurt Johnson and David Robert Ord, *The Coming Interspiritual Age* (Namaste Publishing, 2012). Transforming our changing world through spirituality to survive.
9. Neale Donald Walsch, *Conversations with God* (Hampton Roads, 1997).
10. Watty Piper, The Little Engine That Could (Golden Press, 1979).

For additional HELP (Happiness, Enough, Love, and Peace) take advantage of the Educational Community forever FREE web sites at www.peace.academy and www.worldpeace.academy:

- Awaken to the "normal" addictive disease of our thinking that is about to slay us
- Einstein's solution to prevent human catastrophe and create sustainable peace: *a newer way of thinking* (ANWOT)
- The 7plus2 Formula: 7 word-switches that create ANWOT and 2 secret love creation skills that teach the Golden Rule
- The newer Story of Us: Who are we? What is our mission?
- The Genie Seminar: A newer way of lifetime interactive education to learn what we need to know
- The Mental Freedom Control Panel (MFCP): Eight choices available to our freed will
- The Supreme Law of Orderliness and Predictability
- A Glossary of new symbols and word-switches to sustain ANWOT
- Five expressions of love evolution: egoistic, filial, tribal, erotic, and universal; become a teacher of love creation
- Prevent depression, bullying, and "shooters" (mass killings)
- The genie-like second signaling system that makes us humane becomings and grants our wishes
- This book and two additional free books: *The 7 plus 2 Formula*; *The Stren Collection*
- Call to Action: Become a force for the solution instead of a source of the problem

Summary

People want and need four things to survive and thrive: happiness, enough, love, and peace (HELP). This essay explains the quickest, easiest, most enjoyable and effective way to get them. The puzzle we must solve is "Why do we fill our world with fear, hate, scarcity, and wars?" when we have everything we need to solve the puzzle. Einstein told us the solution: we shall require a newer way of thinking (ANWOT). The seven plus two formula can be made automatic and effortless with thirty days practice. Seven easy-to-learn word substitutions (word switches) create a newer way of thinking; two still secret self-taught skills provide the modern version of the golden rule, "Love ourselves with the abundance that overflows to enrich the world." Make your life really significant! Help create the solution to the biggest puzzle instead or remaining part of the problem. We have become our own worst enemy. Learn how weapons with ultimate destructive power have suddenly made the normal tribal way we think more dangerous than cancer, AIDS, and the Black Death plague. Become one of the one million teachers of Einstein's solution—reach one, reach many. You are needed! Each teacher can pay the seven plus two formula forward to start the domino effect that will circle the world. The easy as one-two-three steps take little time and energy, cost nothing, and will be among your most joyous actions.

The educational community is a nonprofit corporation whose mission is to popularize Einstein's solution to prevent human catastrophe (ANWOT) and create sustainable happiness, love, and world peace (the Golden Rule). All our content is forever free on our websites.

Donald Pet, MD, trained in psychiatry at Johns Hopkins where his favorite mentor was Professor Jerome Frank, world authority on the cause of war and peace. His passion is to popularize Einstein's solution for permanent world peace so his seven grandchildren and humanity can experience the opportunities he has enjoyed.

Printed in the United States
By Bookmasters